THE UNOFFICIAL GUIDE TO THE
EUROVISION
SONG CONTEST

First published in Great Britain in 2023 by Wren & Rook

ISBN: 978 1 5263 6601 6
eBook ISBN: 978 1 5263 6604 7

1 3 5 7 9 10 8 6 4 2

MIX
Paper from
responsible sources
FSC
www.fsc.org   FSC® C104740

Wren & Rook
An imprint of
Hachette Children's Group
Part of Hodder & Stoughton
Carmelite House
50 Victoria Embankment
London EC4Y 0DZ

An Hachette UK Company
www.hachette.co.uk
www.hachettechildrens.co.uk

Printed and bound in Great Britain by Clays Ltd, Elcograf S.p.A.

THE UNOFFICIAL GUIDE TO THE
EUROVISION
SONG CONTEST

wren
&rook

MALCOLM MACKENZIE

CONTENTS

CONTENTS

> Hello, bonsoir, Guten Abend, benvenuto a the Eurovision Song Contest Grand Prix, the greatest show on earth.

EUROVISION:

If you've picked up this book, congratulations, you get douze points. The Eurovision Song Contest is awesome!

It's popular across all of Europe and even in some non-European countries (looking at you, Australia!). But no one loves the contest like the Brits. In 2022, more people watched the Eurovision Song Contest in the UK than in any other country (8.9 million). They love it – but in some countries (halló Iceland) the standom verges on unhinged. Viewing figures regularly show that in Nordic countries, Eurovision is watched by up to 99% of the viewing population. Music is in their blood: it's what keeps it from freezing.

Eurovision is much more than a TV show: it's a way of life, like football or saying you don't eat bread. Since 2015, you can even go to university and study it. But you'll have to travel to Melbourne (where else?) to take Eurovision classes.

After 20 years in the wilderness, the UK is in it to win it!

The contest is much more than a single night of telly viewing. It lasts for at least six months – starting with each country's contestant selection process (some of which are televised, like Spain's Benidorm Fest) and ending with the trophy-snatching on the night of the Grand Final. Add in Junior Eurovision, the Eurovision Choir and the Eurovision Dance Contest, and – well, you get it: it's a whole year of Eurovision fun!

Eurovision has given us megastars like ABBA and Celine Dion, rising stars like Måneskin and Sam Ryder, and personal favourites that everyone else seems to have forgotten, like Lake Malawi and The Common Linnets.

WORLD DOMINATION

Eurovision is a genre. Even if all the songs are utterly different, they share a DNA, a certain sense of pace and drama, a neediness to be liked and, of course, a three-minute run time.

Fans love all of Eurovision: the shoddy and the spectacular, the tear-jerkers and the booty-shakers, the songs with deep impactful messages and the earworms that put 'Baby Shark' to shame – do-do-do-do.

And in this book we're going to cover them all!

Listen up!
The number of songs gifted to us through the contest is now over 1,600. That's one impressive playlist!

All Kinds Of

The contest keeps on giving, becoming increasingly eclectic, getting bigger and better.

Since Eurovision began in 1956, with just seven competing countries, the show has had its ups and downs and even tried the patience of some viewers, like during the four-way tie debacle of 1969. But the best shows survive by evolving – from updating the rules to allow at-home voting to creating must-see TikTok content. There's nothing like it in the world, and to lose it would be Dustin the Turkey levels of terrible. But the great thing about the ESC (Eurovision Song Contest) is that it just takes a couple of great acts to make it iconic. Eurovision is one of the single best ways for a new artist to reach a global audience. And not just for one year, but for a lifetime.

From fairly early on, Eurovision organisers realised that it HAD to be a diverse and inclusive show or suffer from terminal irrelevance and dullness. 1964 saw the first non-white contestant, Indonesian-born Dutch singer Anneke Grönloh, for

Céline Dion,
icon-de-Eurovision

Everything

the Netherlands. Paul Oscar was the first openly gay artist, representing Iceland in 1997, and a year later, trans icon Dana International won. In 2002, Germany sent the first blind performer to the contest, Corinna May, and in 2021, Romania's Eurovision star, Roxen, came out as non-binary. Difference is not a drawback. Eurovision is the perfect place for an artist to celebrate who they are. By its very nature, Eurovision is about belonging and community. Every year it creates a new gang, a troupe who will be linked for ever by their shared experience. As fans, that sense of togetherness is compelling. If you want to get mushy about it, you could call it family.

Eurovision has gone from seven countries having a nice evening out, to a peak of 40 nations battling their way to snatching the gold medal in the Olympics of song. The song is massively important, but let's not pretend it isn't also about crazy fashion, over-the-top performances, impressive vocal ranges, epic dancing, human-sized hamster wheels and pyrotechnics galore. More on all of these later in the book.

What has Eurovision done for us? Quite a lot actually.

- ✓ **1956** Gifted countries with a showcase for their unique talents
- ✓ **1965** Basically taught us French
- ✓ **1967** Made 'no shoes' a thing
- ✓ **1974** Alerted us to the Swedish talent for pop
- ✓ **1975** Educated us in the unfairness of favouritism
- ✓ **1981** Invented 'reveals'
- ✓ **1988** Unleashed the Quebecois Queen
- ✓ **1998** Celebrated trans excellence
- ✓ **2007** Gave drag a global platform, (years before *RuPaul's Drag Race*)
- ✓ **2012** Allowed grannies to bake
- ✓ **2014** Endorsed beards for all
- ✓ **2015** Proved that where you live shouldn't matter between friends
- ✓ **2021** Made rock 'n' roll cool again
- ✓ **2022** Taught us that patience is sometimes rewarded

20 EUROVISION RULES

Thinking of entering the ESC one day? Well, you'd better remember these rules.

1 The song's songwriter has to be from the country; the performer does not.

2 The song must be no longer than three minutes. It has to be original and never before released or publicly performed.

3 Entrants must be sixteen years or over on the day of the final.

4 There can be no more than six performers on stage.

5 No live animals are allowed on stage.

6 No one will fly through the venue on wires.

7 No water is allowed on stage (Jedward put an end to that malarkey with their fountain staging).

8 No confetti is allowed in any performance.

9 There must be no trademarked or overtly poltical or religious content.

10 The song can contain no foul language (Måneskin had to edit their song before they entered it).

11 All lead vocals must be performed live – on stage or off stage.

12 No person on stage is allowed to lip-sync, although pre-recorded background harmonies can be used.

13 No instruments are allowed to be plugged in on stage. All music must be pre-recorded. Instruments can be 'played', for effect, but the music everyone will hear is pre-recorded.

14 44 is the maximum number of countries allowed to enter.

15 26 is the maximum number of songs allowed in the Grand Final. Six are guaranteed – from the Big Five countries and the host nation, the previous year's winner.

16 38 is the maximum number of countries that can compete in the semi-finals for the remaining 20 spots.

17 After a random draw of first half/second half, the running order will be decided by the contest producers.

18 No contestant can participate in more than one entry per year.

19 The dress rehearsal, which the jury judges, must be identical to the final performance.

20 You cannot vote for your own country.

Voting Explained

Each country has a total of 10 votes to give to their favourite 10 songs out of the 26 at the Grand Final. 12 points are awarded to the best song, then 10, 8, 7, 6, 5, 4, 3, 2, and 1. The lesser-liked remaining 16 songs are given no points.

Each national jury, made up of five members from the music industry, will rank all 26 songs in the Grand Final from favourite to least favourite. Their scores will be combined then added to the televotes of viewers at home. The percentage weighting is 50/50.

EUROVISION

52 countries have taken part in Eurovision, not all of them in Europe.

10 former republics of the Soviet Union have competed in the ESC.

Ukraine has an unblemished qualification record, making it to the final with every song they've ever submitted.

Morocco entered just once, in 1980.

Luxembourg is the missing powerhouse of Eurovision. They have won five times, but haven't competed in 30 years.

ICELAND

NORWAY

SWEDEN

FINLAND

RUSSIA

ESTONIA

LA TVIA

LITHUA NIA

IRE LAND

UNI TED KING DOM

DEN MARK

NETHER LANDS

BEL GIUM

LUXEMBURG

GER MA NY

POL AND

BELARUS

CZECH REPUBLIC

UKRAINE

FRA NCE

SWITZERLAND

LIECH TEN STEIN

AUS TRIA

SLOVAKIA

SLOVENIA

HUNGARY

MOLDOVA

PORTUGAL

SPA IN

ANDORA

MONACO

ITALY

SAN MARINO

CROATIA

BOSNIA AND HERZE GOVINA

SERBIA

ROM ANIA

GEORGIA

MONTENEGRO

AL BA NIA

MACE DONIA

BULG ARIA

TURKEY

ARMENIA

GRE E CE

CYPRUS

MOROCCO

MALTA

MAPPED

San Marino almost never qualifies (only ¼ of their songs make it to finals), yet they keep on trying. That's the Eurovision spirit!

Andorra sent six entries to Eurovision between 2004 and 2009. None of them qualified and they seemingly gave up.

AUSTRALIA

ISRAEL

AZERBAIJAN

There are seven countries who have never participated in the contest but are eligible to enter: Algeria, Egypt, Jordan, Lebanon, Libya, Tunisia and Vatican City.

America has broadcast Eurovision every year since 2016. First it was on Logo, then Netflix and most recently Peacock.

The 52 participating countries (and the year they joined)

1. Luxembourg (1956)
2. France (1956)
3. Germany (1956)
4. Italy (1956)
5. Switzerland (1956)
6. Belgium (1956)
7. The Netherlands (1956)
8. Austria (1957)
9. Denmark (1957)
10. United Kingdom (1957)
11. Sweden (1958)
12. Monaco (1959)
13. Norway (1960)
14. Spain (1961)
15. Finland (1961)
16. Yugoslavia (1961)
17. Portugal (1964)
18. Ireland (1965)
19. Malta (1971)
20. Israel (1973)
21. Greece (1974)
22. Turkey (1975)
23. Morocco (1980)
24. Cyprus (1981)
25. Iceland (1986)
26. Bosnia & Herzegovina (1993)
27. Croatia (1993)
28. Slovenia (1993)
29. Estonia (1994)
30. Lithuania (1994)
31. Hungary (1994)
32. Slovakia (1994)
33. Russia (1994)
34. Poland (1994)
35. Romania (1994)
36. North Macedonia (1998)
37. Latvia (2000)
38. Ukraine (2003)
39. Andorra (2004)
40. Albania (2004)
41. Serbia & Montenegro (2004)
42. Belarus (2004)
43. Bulgaria (2005)
44. Moldova (2005)
45. Armenia (2006)
46. Georgia (2007)
47. Serbia (2007)
48. Montenegro (2007)
49. Czech Republic (2007)
50. Azerbaijan (2008)
51. San Marino (2008)
52. Australia (2015)

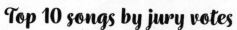

Top 10 songs by jury votes

Artist	Song	Country	Points
Salvador Sobral	Amar Pelos Dois	Portugal	382
Dami Im	Sound of Silence	Australia	320
Sam Ryder	Space Man	UK	283
Kristian Kostov	Beautiful Mess	Bulgaria	278
Cesár Sampson	Nobody but You	Austria	342
Gjon's Tears	Tout l'Univers	Switzerland	267
Cornelia Jakobs	Hold Me Closer	Sweden	258
Benjamin Ingrosso	Dance You Off	Sweden	253
Barbara Pravi	Voilà	France	248
Tamara Todevska	Proud	N Macedonia	247

HIGH AND

Let's break down the highest scoring Eurovision songs: weirdly, some of them aren't even winners.

Top 5 scoring winners (by %)

Artist	Song	Country	Points	% of all possible points
Anne-Marie David	Tu te reconnaîtras	Luxembourg	129	80.63
Brotherhood of Man	Save Your Kisses for Me	UK	164	80.39
Nicole	Ein Bißchen Frieden	Germany	161	78.92
Katrina and the Waves	Love Shine a Light	UK	227	78.82
Alexander Rybak	Fairytale	Norway	387	78.6

Comeback kings

In 2022, 'Fade to Black', Azerbaijan's entry, became the first ever song to get nil-points from the semi-final televote and still make it to the finals off the back of a healthy 96-point jury score.

Nil and void

Up until 2022, there have been 39 instances of nil-points, two in the semi-final and 37 in the Grand Final. Belgium was the first ever recipient of the dreaded zero in 1962. Only one song has ever gotten nil-points from all juries and the public since the new voting system was introduced in 2016: 'Embers' by James Newman, the UK entry for 2021.

Norway and Austria have received the most nil-points ever: 4.

OH, SO LOW

The highest number of 'douze points' ever awarded was given to Kalush Orchestra in 2022, with their song 'Stefania' – 28 of them!!!

Top 10 songs by televote

Artist	Song	Country	Points
Kalush Orchestra	Stefania	Ukraine	439
Salvador Sobral	Amar Pelos Dois	Portugal	376
Sergey Lazarev	You Are the Only One	Russia	361
Kristian Kostov	Beautiful Mess	Bulgaria	337
Jamala	1944	Ukraine	323
Måneskin	Zitti e Buoni	Italy	318
Netta	Toy	Israel	317
KEiiNO	Spirit in the Sky	Norway	291
Go_A	Shum	Ukraine	267
SunStroke Project	Hey Mamma	Moldova	264

The people's winner

The voting public always choose different winners to the jury. The jury loves a serious anthem, while the voters often choose the exciting, quirky and genre-defying songs.

ERAVISION: THE HISTORIC

This is where it all began – as a good-natured competition to bring Europe together after the war.

Despite the fifties being known for their rock 'n' roll (Elvis Presley, Ray Charles, etc), Eurovision of the 1950's was a genteel affair with easy-listening ditties that sound very dated to modern ears. The first ever winner, Lys Assia from Switzerland, and the Netherlands' Corry Brokken, were queens of these golden years, entering three years in a row and each taking home a win.

First

The first ever Eurovision was held in famously neutral Switzerland with a grand total of seven countries: Belgium, France, Germany, Italy, Luxembourg, the Netherlands and Switzerland. Switzerland won . . . maybe they weren't so neutral after all!

Losing is the new winning

Despite coming third in 1958, 'Nel Blu Dipinto Di Blu', aka 'Volare' (To Fly) by Domenico Modugno was the runaway winner of the entire decade. The song went to number one in America, winning two Grammy Awards: Song of the Year and Record of the Year, and it was selected as the second-best Eurovision song of all time at the fiftieth anniversary show in 2005.

First! Eurovision legend
Lys Assia

1950s

Enter the UK . . . just

After missing the first competition, the UK entered with a song so short, that you might've sneezed and missed it. Coming in at 1 minute 52 seconds, 'All', sung by Patricia Bredin, whizzed its way to seventh place, out of ten entries. The song was the first of the competition to be sung in English, and the shortest ever, until Finland broke the record in 2015.

Eurovision started out as a radio show. Cameras did film it for the few people who had televisions but by the sixties, when approximately 75% of homes had a TV set, the show was primarily seen as a television programme.

Apart from the winning song, zero footage survives of the first Eurovision.

1950s WINNERS

Year	Country	Song	Performer
1956	Switzerland	Refrain	Lys Assia
1957	Netherlands	Net als toen	Corry Brokken
1958	France	Dors mon amour	André Claveau
1959	Netherlands	Een beetje	Teddy Scholten

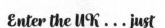

ERAVISION: GO POP!

The swinging sixties took a good five years to reach Eurovision, but when they did, the contest never looked back.

Pop music was pretty much invented in the 1960s, and it finally arrived at Eurovision with France Gall in 1965. The 1960's saw a whole bunch of firsts for the competition, with its first ever broadcast on a Saturday night in 1961, and the first ever nil-points were given in 1962.

> In 1967, Sandie Shaw's 'Puppet on a String' won more than double the points of the runner-up.

The gall of Gainsbourg

France Gall's winning song, Poupée de cire, poupée de son, was the first out-and-out pop song to win Eurovision. The song is cute bubblegum pop, but the lyrics are darker and somewhat worrisome. Written by legendary French singer-songwriter Serge Gainsbourg, the song, which roughly translates to 'Wax Doll, Rag Doll', sees Gall, who was seventeen, singing about how she's only a doll, with a voice controlled by someone else (Gainsbourg) – a little troubling!

1969's four-way tie drama

When four contestants won Eurovision in 1969, it became a whole big thing that scandalised Europe. It's easy to see how it happened. Back then, each jury was made up of ten people who each gave their favourite song one point. So when four countries – France, Spain, the Netherlands and the UK – ended up with 18 points, what could organisers do but 'crown' the lot of them? Luckily there were four medals

BOOM!
Lulu gives the UK its second win

1960s

Only tiny bits of footage of the 1964 show exist. Legend has it that either the Danish broadcaster never actually taped the show or the tapes were destroyed in a fire in the 1970s.

to hand out. It's hard to understand the fuss that was made at the time, but Sweden, Norway, Finland and Portugal were so peeved that they pulled out of the 1970 competition. The European Broadcasting Union (EBU) immediately introduced a tie-break rule, so that it would never happen again, and it hasn't.

The cool kids

To appeal to younger audiences, Eurovision contestants started getting younger. 1964's winner, Gigliola Cinquetti, was only sixteen, the youngest winner until Sandra Kim in 1986. When France Gall won the following year, she was only seventeen. In 1969, Monaco sent twelve-year-old, Jean Jacques – he was pretty good.

Representation in representatives

It took a while, but the mid sixties saw more diverse contestants. Milly Scott, the first black performer, made her debut in 1967, shortly followed by Eduardo Nascimento, representing Portugal, who was the first black male singer to perform.

1960s WINNERS

Year	Country	Song	Performer
1960	France	Tom Pillibi	Jacqueline Boyer
1961	Luxembourg	Nous les amoureux	Jean-Claude Pascal
1962	France	Un premier amour	Isabelle Aubret
1963	Denmark	Dansevise	Grethe and Jørgen Ingmann
1964	Italy	Non Ho L'età	Gigliola Cinquetti
1965	Luxembourg	Poupée de cire, poupée de son	France Gall
1966	Austria	Merci Cherié	Udo Jürgens
1967	UK	Puppet on a String	Sandie Shaw
1968	Spain	La, La, La	Massiel
	UK	Boom Bang-a-Bang	Lulu
	Netherlands	De Troubadour	Lenny Kuhr
1969	France	Un Jour, Un Enfant	Frida Boccara
	Spain	Vivo Cantando	Salomé

ERAVISION: THE CATCHY

The influence of ABBA on the contest cannot be overstated. There is time before the Swedes and a time after.

The shift towards catchy sing-along songs that could be sung by the whole family kicked off in the 1970s. 'Waterloo' changed everything. It might sound quaint to modern ears, but it's a relatively heavy rock song compared to the traditional female soloists who usually won the competition.

Boycott strop

Perhaps due to sour grapes over the four-way-tie of 1969, Sweden, Norway and Finland all boycotted the show in 1970. Portugal also skipped it. Bit petty, but people had a lot of time to sit and fester before the existence of Netflix. This meant that 1970 was a cute affair with only twelve nations competing. A new rule was brought in to stop contestants tying. In the event of a tie, the acts must perform again, with the winner being chosen by a show of hands.

ABBA had the IT factor!

1970s

In 1971, the second and third place countries were also given awards – probably to make up for the 1969 'voting scandal'.

Ireland's 1972 entry 'Ceol an Ghrá' is the only one to ever be sung in Irish.

A south-east feast

The 1970s saw an expansion of countries participating in the contest. Israel joined in 1973 and by the end of the decade had delivered two iconic winners: Izhar Cohen and Alphabeta; and Milk and Honey. In 1974, Greece entered the chat, and a year later in 1975, Turkey were in for a drachma and joined the drama. If you're paying attention, you might have noticed that Israel isn't actually part of Europe, setting a precedent for the EBU extending the hand of friendship for the fun of it.

Voting see-saw

The early seventies saw a new voting system introduced. Each country had two jury members, one who had to be younger than twenty-five years old and one who had to be over twenty-five. They scored each song from 1 to 5. In 1974, national juries of ten people, each with one vote, were introduced. In 1975, the familiar voting pattern of awarding 12 points to the best song, then 10, then 8, down to 1.

'A-Ba-Ni-Bi' was Eurovision's first disco winner. An essential on any playlist!

French hits different

Today we're used to hearing hits sung in Korean, but in the early Eurovision years, it was French. Eurovision rules stated that you had to sing in one of your country's languages so half the songs were sung in French, giving French songs a much better chance of success.

1970s WINNERS

Year	Country	Song	Performer
1970	Ireland	All Kinds of Everything	Dana
1971	Monaco	Un banc, un arbre, une rue	Séverine
1972	Luxembourg	Après toi	Vicky Leandros
1973	Luxembourg	Tu te reconnaîtras	Anne-Marie David
1974	Sweden	Waterloo	ABBA
1975	Netherlands	Ding-a-Dong	Teach-In
1976	UK	Save Your Kisses for Me	Brotherhood of Man
1977	France	L'oiseau et l'enfant	Marie Myriam
1978	Israel	A-Ba-Ni-Bi	Izhar Cohen and Alphabeta
1979	Israel	Hallelujah	Milk and Honey

ERAVISION:
THE CHEESE-TASTIC

Eurovision in the eighties was full of bouncy tunes and power ballads – almost as big as the shoulder pads and the hairstyles!

The eighties were peak Eurovision! The costumes, the hairstyles, the dance routines – everything was geared towards making the show a big, dramatic event and not just a singing competition. The nostalgia is strong for this decade.

ABBA hangover

Post-ABBA, groups were big winners in the eighties, with the likes of Bucks Fizz, Herreys and Bobbysocks!. They copied ABBA's success with jaunty songs and fashions to match. The lyrics weren't that deep and the songs were all geared towards the dance floor – or at least your bedroom carpet.

The voice

As a rule, Eurovision is about performing a great song, not having a massive voice. When Celine won in 1988, she was a sign of the changing times. The power of her voice was a shock, and surely helped cement her win. Not many can compete with the Canadian's one-in-a-generation vocal cords.

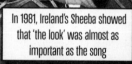

In 1981, Ireland's Sheeba showed that 'the look' was almost as important as the song

Weirdly, the UK was drawn to perform after Norway six years in a row, from 1981 to 1986.

1980s

16, unlucky for some

In 1986, Iceland decided enough was enough, and finally decided to join the Eurovision party. They were rewarded with 16th place not once, not twice, but three years in a row from 1986 to 1988. Then, to make matters even worse, in 1989, they came 22nd – last place with nil-points. Unbelievably, they have yet to win. Could this be their year?

Do you know where the UK hosted the contest in 1982? Harrogate in North Yorkshire.

Bucks Fizz were formed with the sole purpose of winning the Eurovision Song Contest.

UK still OK

In the eighties, the UK was a major contender at the contest, placing in the top ten every year bar one. From 1981 to 1984, their songs were radio-friendly and fun but by 1985, something in the UK selection process had changed and the songs were less peppy, perhaps to appease ageing Eurovision judges. Despite decent placings at the contest the Eurovision entries had mixed success on the top 40 singles chart. This left the competition wide open for Ireland's, Johnny Logan to make an impressive comeback in 1987.

1980s WINNERS

Year	Country	Song	Performer
1980	Ireland	What's Another Year	Johnny Logan
1981	UK	Making Your Mind Up	Bucks Fizz
1982	Germany	Ein Bißchen Frieden	Nicole
1983	Luxembourg	Si la vie est Cadeau	Corinne Hermès
1984	Sweden	Diggi-Loo Diggi-Ley	Herreys
1985	Norway	La det swinge	Bobbysocks!
1986	Belgium	J'aime la vie	Sandra Kim
1987	Ireland	Hold Me Now	Johnny Logan
1988	Switzerland	Ne partez pas sans moi	Celine Dion
1989	Yugoslavia	Rock Me	Riva

ERAVISION: THE SLIGHTLY 'MEH'

There was a lot to love in the nineties, and arguably even more to forget.

Were the nineties dull? The decade that brought us grunge, Britpop, R'n'B and hip hop, Take That and the Spice Girls and it was full of bangers. But where was that at Eurovision? Nowhere to be found.

Is Gina G the most robbed contestant ever?

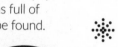

Did you know that Gina G's sparkly dress was originally made for Cher?

Ooh ah, not even second

In 1996, Gina G's 'Ooh Aah . . . Just a Little Bit' came eighth. Forget everything else, this is arguably the biggest scandal in Eurovision history. How on earth did a song that was a genuine hit around the world, number 12 in America, number 5 in Australia and number 1 in the UK, fail to pick up more votes? Perhaps the vocals weren't the strongest on the night, but something had to be going on with the voting juries. What's the bet that a televoting public would've made this their winner? Shame televoting didn't come in until 1997.

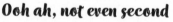

1990s

Having a Ball

Bless him, national treasure Michael Ball gave it a good go in 1992, coming second with a solid tune, 'One Step Out of Time'. The next year, Sonia suffered the same fate, coming second with 'Better the Devil You Know'. Being the runner-up was something the UK had grown accustomed to, but that would all come to an end after Imaani's gorgeous 'Where Are You' in 1999.

Katrina and the Waves had the biggest Eurovision winning song of the nineties, winning by a landslide to receive the most points of any Eurovision song – 227.

Ireland, douze points

Ireland was always winning in the nineties, and even though the songs were good, looking back, it does make the decade seem a bit dull. But there were two that stood out. One was 'In Your Eyes', a timeless classic that could've come from any of the preceding three decades. Niamh Kavanagh had a wonderfully smooth and soulful voice, but she was styled like a middle-aged parishioner and you'd be forgiven for thinking she was a much older. Three years later Eimear Quinn of Rivendell – sorry, Dublin – won with 'The Voice', a very ethereal and very Irish entry that sounds as good today as it did in 1996.

Televoting was trialled for the first time in 1997.

1990s WINNERS

Year	Country	Song	Performer
1990	Italy	Insieme: 1992	Toto Cutugno
1991	Sweden	Fångad av en Stormvind	Carola
1992	Ireland	Why Me	Linda Martin
1993	Ireland	In Your Eyes	Niamh Kavanagh
1994	Ireland	Rock 'n' Roll Kids	Paul Harrington and Charlie McGettigan
1995	Norway	Nocturne	Secret Garden
1996	Ireland	The Voice	Eimear Quinn
1997	UK	Love Shine a Light	Katrina and the Waves
1998	Israel	Diva	Dana International
1999	Sweden	Take Me to Your Heaven	Charlotte Nilsson

ERAVISION:
THE TRASHY NOUGHTIES

Lordi they were good

There were some amazing highs and some abysmal lows, but Eurovision in the noughties was never boring.

When you think of the noughties, you might think of the absymal performances of the UK. Jemini gave the UK their first ever nil-points in 2003, Daz Sampson's 'Teenage Life' in 2006 did not give anyone life, and Scooch were almost funny in 2007, but the laughter was silenced in 2008 by Andy 'the bin man'.

Vote of no confidence

Televoting was introduced for some countries in 1997, and by 2004, it was the sole method of calculating scores, with juries being axed entirely. The format made the shows more interactive, but it also meant that acts increasingly appealed to the public with eye-catching outfits and crazy antics until, in some cases, the song was the last thing you remembered about a performance. Yes, we mean you, Latvia's Pirates of the Sea (2008).

Semis, finally

The introduction of semi-finals was essential with all the new countries wanting to participate in the competition. By 2004, there were 36 entrants. The introduction of the semis meant that Eurovision was no longer a single-day affair, but a two-day event and then, by 2009, a three-day extravaganza.

The 2000 contest was the first to be broadcast live on the internet.

The 1000th song of the contest was performed by Brian Kennedy for Ireland in 2006.

2000s

The feast from the east

It didn't take the former Yugoslav and Soviet states long to find their footing at Eurovision, and by the noughties, they weren't just sending good songs, they were winning. Half of the winners of the decade came from Eastern Europe.
In this decade, none of the Big Five or any of the founding countries won. The influx of new talent meant that it was harder than ever to win the contest, but with more songs to sing and dance to every year, the fans are all winners.

The audience of 35,000 in Copenhagen in 2001 is the largest ever gathered for the contest.

In 2008, a record 43 countries took part in the contest.

Eurovision is not a joke

A year before Andriy Mykhailovych Danylko made Eurovision history with his drag character Verka Serduchka, Icelandic comedian Ágústa Eva Erlendsdóttir brought her obnoxious fictitious persona Silvía Night (think Borat crossed with Barbie) to Eurovision with the song 'Congratulations'. The satirical song, which originally featured swearing, was booed when it was performed at the semi-final and did not make it to the Grand Final.

2000s WINNERS

Year	Country	Song	Performer
2000	Denmark	Fly on the Wings of Love	Olsen Brothers
2001	Estonia	Everybody	Tanel Padar, Dave Benton and 2XL
2002	Latvia	I Wanna	Marie N
2003	Turkey	Everyway That I Can	Sertab Erener
2004	Ukraine	Wild Dances	Ruslana
2005	Greece	My Number One	Helena Paparizou
2006	Finland	Hard Rock Hallelujah	Lordi
2007	Serbia	Molitva	Marija Šerifović
2008	Russia	Believe	Dima Bilan
2009	Norway	Fairytale	Alexander Rybak

ERAVISION:
THE UTTERLY ICONIC

When we talk about the best Eurovision years and songs, they mostly come from this decade.

Now you're talking! All Eurovision is good Eurovision, but not all Eurovisions are created equal. Loreen's win in 2012 signposted a new dawn, which would take Eurovision up, up, up, up, up, uuuuup.

Since Ell & Nikki's win, mixed-sex groups have gone from strength to strength

I got new rules

In 2013, the running order rules were changed so that it was no longer totally random. Where the host country performs is still drawn at random, but everyone else goes into a pot to decide if they'll perform in the first or second half. Then the producers decide where in the first or second half each act will go.

Swedey darling

Ja! You guessed it. Sweden were the most successful country of the decade, with eight top 10 positions and two wins. They placed third twice, with Eric Saade and Sanna Nielsen, and fifth three times, with Frans, Robin Bengtsson and John Lundvik. From 2014 to 2019 not a single song Sweden entered scored less than 200 points.

Did 2019 have the highest quality of songs ever? Duncan Laurence deserved the trophy, but in a less competitive year, Mahmood would've been a brilliant, memorable winner. Ditto KEiiNO, Kate Miller-Heidke, John Lundvik . . .

2010s

2011: *Anyone's year*

2011 was a lukewarm or fun year depending on how you look at it, because everyone was doing well and when voting began it seemed like anyone's game. Even Switzerland, who came last, did so with a respectable 19 points. The UK and Ireland performed fairly decently for a change, with household names Blue and Jedward each scoring in triple figures: 100 and 119 respectively.

Gender equality

Historically, female winners of Eurovision have outnumbered men, but by the 2010s that had started to shift, and now it's impossible to say if the girls have the edge, or the boys for that matter, because it's a pretty balanced split. Mixed groups like Madame Monsieur, The Common Linnets, Daði and Gagnamagnið, The Roop and Go_A seem to be more popular than ever. The ABBA influence strikes again.

Portugal's controversial winner

After giving Portugal their very first win in 2017, Salvador Sobral did something even more shocking – he bad-mouthed Eurovision. Not directly, but how else could fans interpret his winning Debbie Downer speech? 'We live in a world of disposable music without any content,' he said. Jaw drop. Mic drop. No fireworks? No Eurovision.

2010s WINNERS

Year	Country	Song	Performer
2010	Germany	Satellite	Lena
2011	Azerbaijan	Running Scared	Ell & Nikki
2012	Sweden	Euphoria	Loreen
2013	Denmark	Only Teardrops	Emmelie de Forest
2014	Austria	Rise Like a Phoenix	Conchita Wurst
2015	Sweden	Heroes	Måns Zelmerlöw
2016	Ukraine	1944	Jamala
2017	Portugal	Amar Pelos Dois	Salvador Sobral
2018	Israel	Toy	Netta
2019	Netherlands	Arcade	Duncan Laurence

ERAVISION: THE ROARRRRING

Right now, Eurovision has never been cooler and its songs are reaching bigger audiences than ever before.

When TikTok was announced as a media partner for the 2022 Eurovision Song Contest, it solidified a change that had, honestly, been coming for a while. The new social media platforms pairing with the old-timer of music shows might seem like an unlikely partnership, until you realise that a huge chunk of Eurovision's audience is under twenty-five. The show is embracing evolution while keeping camp chaos at its core.

Rosa Linn snaps TikTok

Once upon a time, coming 20th at Eurovision would have been a failure. But guess what? It doesn't have to be like that. In 2022, Armenia's 'Snap' by Rosa Linn was beaten by 19 other songs, but it went on to become the biggest Eurovision hit of the year, finding a massive wave of love on TikTok with hundreds of millions of views. 'Snap' then entered the UK and US charts and saw Rosa Linn shoot to fame.

Edge of glory

Eurovision loves a big ballad, and songs like Duncan Laurence's 'Arcade' are obviously going to connect with audiences, but that was in 2019.

Rosa Linn, Armenia's first winner, sorta, kinda

2020s

Måneskin were the first band to win Eurovision since Lordi in 2006.

'The Big Five' are making comebacks! In 2021 and 2022, Italy won; France, the UK and Spain all performed better than they had in over two decades; and Germany – well, Germany came 25th both years. Could 2023 be their year to turn things around?

So far, the 2020s have brought two of the edgiest winners in the history of the contest. Måneskin's 'Zitti e Buoni' was a non-ironic all-out rock anthem that has turned the Italians into one of the world's biggest rock groups, while 'Stefania' by Kalush Orchestra was the first winning rap track. Will this new direction last? What style of music will the next winner perform?

UK back on track

Along with America, South Korea and Sweden, the UK is a world leader when it comes to music, so it's very frustrating that they've performed so badly over the last two decades. Until 2022, when Sam Ryder's 'Space Man' proved the UK could have a hit!

The lost year

When 2020's Eurovision was cancelled, all of the songs and acts were already prepared to perform, so organisers put on a non-competitive showcase called the Eurovision Song Celebration 2020. If you've not watched it yet, boy are you in for a treat!

2020s WINNERS SO FAR

Year	Country	Song	Performer
2020	N/A	Contest cancelled due to COVID pandemic	
2021	Italy	Zitti e Buoni	Måneskin
2022	Ukraine	Stefania	Kalush Orchestra

BEST & WORST POSITIONS

The best song can win from any spot in the show's running order, but some spots seem to be luckier than others.

The last winners to perform in the first half of the show were Kalush Orchestra in 2022 and Duncan Laurence in 2019. They both performed 12th, almost at the halfway point of the show. Before that, 'first-half winners' performed in 11th (Jamala), 10th (Måns Zelmerlöw), 11th (Conchita Wurst) and 10th (Ruslana).

17

The luckiest spot to be in. More winners have performed 17th than any other: seven in total, including Loreen and Lordi.

The last time a song won after being performed in the first nine acts was two decades ago. Turkey won in 2003 in fourth position.

Most winners

Approximately two thirds of winners perform in the second half of the show. In fact, from 2005 to 2013 every winner performed in the second half of the show.

2

The famously cursed spot to perform in. No second song of the night has ever won.

First!

Three acts have won after performing first, and weirdly they're all groups with fairly similar songs: 'Ding-A-Dong' (1975), 'Save Your Kisses for Me' (1976) and 'Diggi-Loo Diggi-Ley' (1984).

Lucky 20s

Since the year 2000, performing towards the end of the show in 20th to 24th position has been the best place to be. Eight winners have come from these spots.

INTERVAL ACTS

Chaotic doesn't even begin to describe some of the half-time acts.

How do you put on a half-time show like the Superbowl when your entire production is a 'half-time show'? You have to be even bigger and even more jaw-dropping – as it turns out, often for all the wrong reasons.

Justin Timberlake

In 2016, Justin Timberlake's performance of 'Rock Your Body' and 'Can't Stop the Feeling' was pretty good, but seeing the global mega-star cosy up to Eurovision hero, Måns Zerlmerlöw during an interview segment was even better.

The Wombles

The 1974 half-time breather was provided by popular children's TV stars The Wombles. If that sounds ridiculous, bear in mind that The Wombles had four top 10 hits in 1974. FOUR!!!

Boyzone

Between 1996 and 1998, Irish boyband Boyzone had six number 1 hits in the UK, so they were a natural choice for the interval act in 1997. Sadly, the fivesome did not sing one of their massive hits, but the sombre ballad, 'Let the Message Run Free', which wasn't even a single. Why?

Madonna

Queen of pop, Madonna, at Eurovision? It should've been a joyously magical joining of forces. It wasn't. While not without its moments, the 2019 performance was ultimately an underwhelming, self-indulgent buzzkill and not the riotous celebration we deserved.

Aqua

The band most famous for the unforgettable song 'Barbie Girl' gave Eurovision an unforgettable interval medley of their greatest hits in 2001. Perhaps wanting to shake their shiny pop image, during the intro to their iconic single, singer Lene, aka 'Barbie', told bandmate René, aka 'Ken', to get lost – except she used a four-letter swear word. Yikes! Not on brand for Eurovision.

10 ICONIC MOMENTS

Just some of the moments that live rent-free in the brains of millions.

1

When *ABBA* won in 1974, Eurovision instantly became a launchpad to global superstardom.

3

Lordi brought an injection of irreverent chaos to the show at a time when it was becoming too predictably safe and bubblegum.

2

When the *Bucks Fizz* boys ripped the long skirts off the girls to reveal shorter skirts, to the lyric, 'and if you wanna see some more', it was historic and for some, a bit scandalous.

4

With her instantly identifiable cartoon look, 2007 runner-up *Verka Serduchka* has pretty much become the unofficial mascot of the competition.

5 The 'Russian grannies', **Buranovskiye Babushki** are proof that you're never too old to live your dream. They came second to Loreen.

6 Poor **Mariya Yaremchuk**: we don't remember you, only your hamster wheel.

7 **Francesco Gabbani** sang philosophy to an ape in 2017, but the weirdest thing is that he probably should've won. What a song.

8 **Daði & Gagnamagnið** and their weird geeky dancing was a hundred percent relatable content. They performed in the 2020 showcase and their song 'Think About Things', was one of the most popularly streamed that year.

9 Serbia's **Konstrakta** washed her hands and made hygiene mesmerising. Very on brand for the 2022 COVID competition.

10 The single best hosting moment has to be the performance of 'Love, Love Peace, Peace' by Swedish Eurovision presenter **Petra Mede** and **Måns Zelmerlöw** in Stockholm in 2016. If you want the ESC explained in four and a half minutes: YouTube it.

Eurovision Style:

Fashion is subjective, but some outfits feel the pull of landfill more than others.

There are so many memorable Eurovision style moments, from shoeless Sandie Shaw and Loreen to the tinfoil fantasies of Verka and Jedward. If you don't see your faves here, turn the page for even more showstoppers.

BEST
Go_A, Ukraine 2021
Dramatic fashion muppet

BEST
Dami Im, Australia, 2016
Totally wedded to this look

WURST
Jamie-Lee, Germany, 2016
Crazy, kooky, annoying

WURST
Olivia Newton-John, UK, 1974
Nana's spare room bedspread looks well itchy

The best and wurst

WURST
InCulto, Lithuania, 2010
Businessman meets toddler pageant

BEST
Tamta, Cyprus, 2019
Wipe-clean PVC is perfect for messy eaters

WURST
Gipsy, Czech Republic, 2009
Marvel Cinematic Universe aerobics instructor

BEST
Conchita Wurst, Austria, 2014
Gold fishtail eleganza – a look you win in

ICON AWARD
Herreys, Sweden, 1984
The Herreys' 'golden shoes' all but won the Eurovision Song Contest for them in 1984. Icons – all six of them

EVOLUTION OF THE
GINORMO-DRESS

European Broadcasting Union: You have three minutes to make an impression Contestants: Challenge accepted.

Linda Wagenmakers, Netherlands, 2000
If Eurovision is a circus, I'm the tent.

Aminata, Latvia, 2015
A genuinely gorgeous homage to Diana Ross.

Kate Miller-Heidke, Australia, 2019
We know she's from Oz, but we didn't expect Kate to come as Glinda the good witch.

Manizha,
Russia, 2021
Perfection has a name
and it's Manizha.
The best Eurovision
reveal of all time?

Aliona Moon,
Moldova, 2013
The galaxy trend was
huge in 2013.
Not as big as this
skirt though.

Elina Nechayeva,
Portgual, 2018
Isabella from
Encanto is real
and impossibly
beautiful.

Hairography

Category is: let your hair do the moving while you do the singing.

An old Russian proverb states that if you tie the hair of twins together you win the Eurovision Song Contest. Of course it's not true: **The Tolmachevy Sisters** came seventh.

A really long plait like **Slavko Kalezić's** is an attention-grabber and – whisper it – a nasty weapon if any judge gives you nil-points.

Wow! So much hair! **Eleni Foureira** had hair so animated that a cartoon rendering of Portugal's 2018 entry would take Pixar artists a year before they even reached the first 'yeah-ah, yeah-ah.'

When **Bilal** sang 'Roi' at the Eurovision final, it was the day before the *Game of Thrones* finale. Of course, he went as Gen Z Khaleesi.

It would be easy to say that Serbia's 2021 entry, **Hurricane,** look like they've been caught in a hurricane . . . so let's say that.

Nothing projects the image of a winner like a braided crown of hair. Israel's **Eden Alene** knew what she was doing.

Ethan's hair is so silky. The whole band have great hair. **Måneskin** should do shampoo adverts.

Super-long hair on men is shorthand for 'I'm committed to rock'n'roll'. **Sam Ryder** is the real deal. He's not putting that ravishing hair in a greasy net to flip burgers.

EL DIABLO VS

Loreen's low-key witchy vibes made her a winner in 2012.

Inga and Anush representing Armenia cast a spell on the Eurovision audience in Moscow in 2009.

Eurovision fans were bats about Finnish rockers Lordi in 2006.

FALLEN ANGELS

Heaven and hell are permanent features at Eurovision (in the songs and looks).

Ukraine's Mika Newton: voice of an angel, looks like an angel, song literally called 'Angel'.

Norway's Tix did the whole angel thing in 2021. He sang about fighting demons and came 18th. Time to retire this aesthetic from the mood board?

In 2015, Poland's Monika Kuszyńska was all white on the night.

Questionable Looks

Dance costumes you'd never wear anywhere.

In 2009, Dita Von Teese wore a veil to perform with Alex Swings Oscar Sings!, but she was even harder to spot dressed as a beetroot on ITV's *The Masked Dancer* in 2021.

Iconic bonkers alert! When Poland's Donatan & Cleo had a woman churning butter on stage, did it make sense? No. Is Eurovision supposed to make sense? Also, no.

EINS, ZWEI, DREI

Sing live AND dance, are you mad? Yeah, of course. This is Eurovision.

Eurovision is a show; you can't just stand there. OK – you can just stand there, but even a serious singer like Barbara Pravi waved her arms about. Here are 10 ways to make your performance pop!

STEP

If Steps (and TikTok) have proved anything, it's that a good dance routine sells a song. In 2021, Natalia Gordienko took some basic steps and turned them into exactly the sort of thing you want to learn after four hours of partying.

RUMP

Shake it like Ani Lorak, but careful you don't take an eye out with the beaded fringe.

JUMP

Got questionable rhythm like Jedward? Just jump around – a lot, and really, really high.

ARMS

If you have nice toned arms like Alyona Lanskaya, do the least with them while everyone makes like the goddess Kali behind you.

LIFT

You're the star. Make someone pick you up and carry you around like Justin Bieber at the Great Wall of China. Edurne García Almagro did, and there's not a bead of sweat on her.

DANCING

CRAB
Show off those yoga moves like Cyprus star Elena Tsagkrinou.

FLIP
In 2015, Moldova's Eduard Romanyuta casually backflipped. Because we all know it's that easy.

FLAP
Destiny's handography was giving Charleston flapper, vogue ball realness – and those exercises you have to do after nine hours on your phone.

BOPS
Miki closed out the 2019 contest because his song 'La Venda' was the perfect bop to close the show; so what if he finished 22nd?

LEAN
The leany dance from Germany's Jendrik is a proper cheeky chappie. Give it a go when you're feeling low . . .

Totally Floored

They're not lazy, it's part of the show.

Traditionally, singers of ballads would get off their stool mid-song to add drama. In recent years, artists have decided to up their game by rolling around on the floor before they stand up. Thank goodness for anti-bac wipes.

2008

Russia's Dima Bilan is the definition of too much. He was on his knees, on his back, cross-legged, on his feet, then back to his knees. In the words of 2019 Twitter: we stan.

2017

Levina lay down specifically for a cool camera trick which seemingly zooms in on her from a mile away in the sky.

2022

Cornelia Jakobs of Sweden started 'Hold Me Closer' on the floor, then got up when the beat kicked in. A real pro: that's how you do it.

2021

At first, it looked like Elena Tsagkrinou's time on the ground was a little pre-show stretch, but she found her way back there for some more dramatic moves.

2018

Ieva spent too long plonked on the floor – two full minutes – and because the song isn't very exciting either, she failed to make the final.

2013

Emmelie de Forest lent vulnerability to her winning performance by starting seated then finding the strength to face the wind machine and get up.

10 TIMES THE NO-POLITICS RULE WAS BROKEN

We're regularly told that politics have no place in Eurovision, and to that we say: as if!

1968
General Franco, the fascist dictator of Spain, was accused of bribing judges all over Europe to gain extra points for his country, especially in 1968, the year Spain beat the UK's Cliff Richard by one point.

1973
Israeli–Palestinian tensions were so high during Israel's first ever performance that there were rumours Israel's contestant Ilanit wore a bulletproof vest to perform.

1978
When Jordan broadcast Eurovision for the first time in 1978, they switched the TV signal off during Israel's performance and when it looked like Israel were going to win.

2009
Georgia's 'We Don't Wanna Put In' was disqualified. Say the last part of the song title quickly and you'll understand why.

2014
There was so much booing during Russia's entry from the Tolmachevy Sisters, that the following year in Vienna, 'anti-booing technology' was introduced.

2018
Turkey boycotted Eurovision because it was 'too gay'. Hungary followed Turkey's example and announced in 2019 that they were pulling out of future competitions for the same reason. Bye, girl, bye!

2019
Openly gay singer Bilal received a lot of hate before the contest in Tel Aviv due to his colourful appearance and sexuality.

2019
Icelandic entrants Hatari held up Palestinian flags in support of Palestine in the Palestinian–Israeli conflict during the contest in Israel. The Icelandic TV company was fined €5,000.

2021
It was widely reported that officials in Malta's government were placing bets on Destiny, to make her favourite to win, which would increase the attention brought to the song 'Je me casse' and therefore increase its chances of winning.

2022
The vote-rigging scandal of 2022 will go down in Eurovision history. When six countries were curiously all seen to be voting for each other in the semi-finals, their scores were removed and they were disqualified from voting in the Grand Final.

DIARY OF A

Winning the Eurovision Song Contest is the easy part; you've got to get on the show first!

Want to know exactly how a Eurovision performance comes together? Well, according to the big cheese show organiser, Twan van de Nieuwenhuijzen, it's actually a lot quicker than you might think.

1 The song delivery deadline is at the **end of March.**

2 Each nation's delegation sends their chosen song recording, complete with a 'look and feel' document explaining the concept they're after in terms of staging. Video clips and images are often included.

3 After the packages have been viewed by the ESC team, each nation's delegation has **20 minutes** to explain their plans for the staging in real life.

4 Lighting and LED creatives and directors of the show start work on making it happen.

5 The in-house Eurovision show-makers make one-camera-angle videos of how each song would look, including dancers and props.

6 The ESC does stand-in rehearsals with professionals and sends a link with the video to each delegation country.

EUROVISION PERFORMANCE

7 The countries have **24 hours** to give their feedback on the rehearsal.

8 The country delegations fly to the host nation.

9 The ESC team makes adjustments based on feedback.

10 First rehearsals in person begin.

11 After three runs of their act, performers head to the viewing room, where performers watch the performance back for the first time.

12 They have **20 minutes** to discuss any changes with muti-cam directors.

13 And that's it. Tweaks and adjustments are hopefully then kept to a minimum.

14 The ESC then chooses the running order based on what would be best for the show, with surprises for a massively varied audience. They take into consideration contrasting musical styles, numbers of performers, languages and the look, plus practical things like massive props and staging. Transitions need to be doable in **35 seconds**.

STORY OF A WINNING SONG:
'ZITTI E BUONI'
BY MÅNESKIN

With approximately 10 billion views on TikTok, Måneskin have shown that with the right song and the right artist, Eurovision contestants can conquer the world!

2021's winning song was a gamechanger. Eurovision had been on an upward swing ever since Loreen won in 2012, but Måneskin did the impossible: they single-handedly made Eurovision cool. Something nobody in 60+ years had managed to do. Like ABBA, 47 years before them, the foursome have gone on to became one of the biggest bands on the planet.

Saviours of rock

Since winning Eurovision, Måneskin have attracted the attention of rock fans all over the world. By 2022, the average number of streams per month of their Eurovision winning song on Spotify hit 38 million. That's more than established rock gods The Rolling Stones (21 million), Metallica (18 million) and David Bowie (15 million). "Seeing our numbers grow so much in such a short space of time is crazy," Victoria admitted in a 2022 interview with *Kerrang!* "especially considering that some of the songs are in Italian."

'Rock and roll never dies.'

– Damiano David

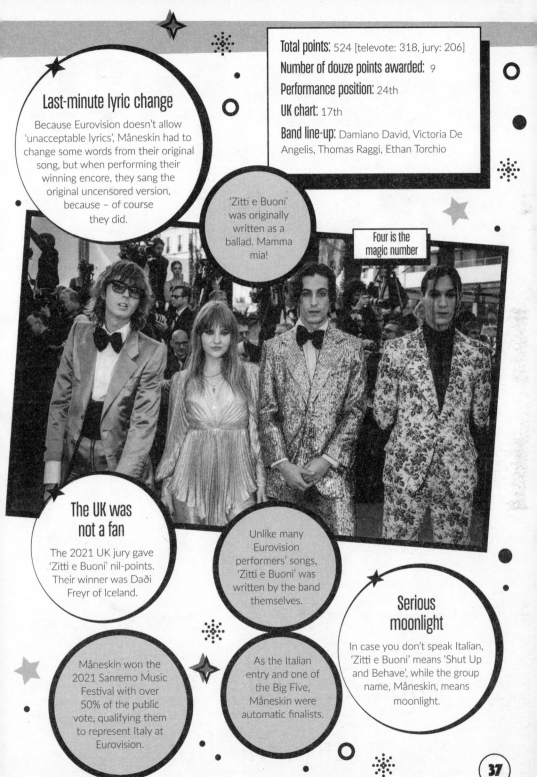

Last-minute lyric change

Because Eurovision doesn't allow 'unacceptable lyrics', Måneskin had to change some words from their original song, but when performing their winning encore, they sang the original uncensored version, because – of course they did.

'Zitti e Buoni' was originally written as a ballad. Mamma mia!

Four is the magic number

Total points: 524 [televote: 318, jury: 206]

Number of douze points awarded: 9

Performance position: 24th

UK chart: 17th

Band line-up: Damiano David, Victoria De Angelis, Thomas Raggi, Ethan Torchio

The UK was not a fan

The 2021 UK jury gave 'Zitti e Buoni' nil-points. Their winner was Daði Freyr of Iceland.

Unlike many Eurovision performers' songs, 'Zitti e Buoni' was written by the band themselves.

Serious moonlight

In case you don't speak Italian, 'Zitti e Buoni' means 'Shut Up and Behave', while the group name, Måneskin, means moonlight.

Måneskin won the 2021 Sanremo Music Festival with over 50% of the public vote, qualifying them to represent Italy at Eurovision.

As the Italian entry and one of the Big Five, Måneskin were automatic finalists.

DOUZE FACTS

Because knowledge is power ... especially at a Eurovision quiz!

1

In 2022, Sam Ryder won the jury vote with 283 points: more jury votes than the winning act, Stefania, who only received 192. The Ukrainian act did go on to win the competition with a landslide 439 televotes.

2

The 'Eurovision Anthem' that opens the ESC every year is 'Prelude to Te Deum' by Marc-Antoine Charpentier.

3

When Kalush Orchestra won the contest in 2022, they were the first all-male group to win since Herreys in 1984. We know what you're thinking – Lordi had a female member, Miss Awa.

4

Salvador Sobral's winning song, 'Amar Pelos Dois', was written and produced by his sister Luisa Sobral, and when he won, he brought her on stage to sing the reprise performance with him.

5

'Nocturne' by Secret Garden, from Norway, won the contest in 1995 with the fewest words in a winning song: 24.

7

Between 1956 and 1998, every song was accompanied by a live orchestra. Backing tracks were introduced in 1999. Imagine an orchestral Måneskin!

8

San Marino can't televote because their phones are part of the Italian network.

6

Winners returning to perform at the contest for two consecutive years became a thing with Johnny Logan in 1988.

9

Nicole's 1982 winning song 'Ein Bißchen Frieden' is the only Eurovision winner to go to number one in every European country it was released in.

10

Benny from ABBA wrote a song for Norway in 1981 and it got nil-points.

12

The maximum 'douze points' that a country can give another was introduced in 1975. The first country to receive 12 points was serial winner Luxembourg.

11

While they were in the competition, Luxembourg was the country to beat. They won twice in the sixties, twice in the seventies and once in the eighties. Weirdly, none of their singers were from Luxembourg. Four were French and one was Greek.

COUNTRY ROADS:
UNITED KINGDOM

The UK went from being a constant contender to the biggest flop.

1957
Patricia Bredin

The UK's first entry was in Eurovision's second year: Patricia Bredin with the song 'All'. She came seventh out of 10 entries.

1959
Seconds to go!

From 1959 to 1961, the UK came second three times in a row.

1960
Host with the most

The UK hosted Eurovision for the first time seven years before they even won. The UK stepped in when the Netherlands didn't want to host again after having hosted in 1958.

1967
Sandie Shaw

Sandie was Britain's first winner, with 'Puppet on a String'. She began an 11-year run where every song the UK sent to Eurovision made it to the top 4.

1968
Cliff Richard

The UK probably should've won with 'Congratulations', but Cliff Richard's song lost out to Spain's Massiel by one point. But it still gave Cliff his seventh number 1 of the sixties, so congrats for that.

1969
Lulu

The infamous four-way tie saw 'Boom Bang-a-Bang by Lulu win for the UK with 18 points.

The UK has hosted the contest more times than any other country: nine times including 2023.

1976
Brotherhood of Man

The UK performed first on the night and still managed to win, that's how good their song 'Save Your Kisses For Me' was. It is likely the biggest-selling Eurovision winning song of all time – 6 million copies sold!

1981
Buck's Fizz

Another two-boy, two-girl group, like ABBA, Buck's Fizz won the contest with 'Making Your Mind Up'. The song was huge, selling 4 million copies worldwide.

1996
Gina G

'Ooh Aah . . . Just A Little Bit' came 8th. That's still a shockingly low placing for one of the most memorable entries of all time. Not only was the song a UK number 1, it's one of the biggest Eurovision hits in America, reaching 12 on the Billboard chart – something no Eurovision song has achieved since.

1997
Katrina and the Waves

'Love Shine a Light' was the highest-scoring UK song until Sam Ryder: 227 points. 'Love Shine a Light' was an even bigger hit for Katrina and the Waves than 'Walking on Sunshine', getting to number 3 in the UK singles chart.

2002
Jessica Garlick

When Jessica came third in 2002, she was the first of only three UK acts of the twenty-first century to land in the top 10. The other two were Jade Ewen and Sam Ryder.

2003
Noughties

The UK received nil-points for the first time in 2003 and they deserved it. Jemini's 'Cry Baby' was a tear-inducingly average attempt at a Steps B-side.

2022
Sam Ryder

Sam Ryder single-handedly took away the pain of a decade outside the top 10 with 'Space Man', a song that, despite coming second, gave the UK its most points ever.

2012
Hump day

The UK loves to complain about 'political voting', but when Sweden sent Loreen and they sent Engelbert Humperdinck, a man whose biggest hit had been over 40 years ago, guess who was going to win?

THEY ARE THE HEROES OF OUR TIME . . .
CELINE DION

Is Celine the biggest superstar to pass through Eurovision? Peut-être.

Celine Dion is one of the biggest-selling artists of all time, with one of the most recognisable voices in music – and on top of that, she's a proper hoot.

Before Eurovision

She might not have been globally famous when she won Eurovision, but in her native Quebec, Canada, Celine was very well known. She released her first French language album in 1981, at the age of thirteen, and by the time she was singing for Switzerland in 1988, she had released eight albums. Her manager, René Angélil, believed in her talent so much that he mortgaged his house to pay for her first record, and eventually he even married her. Now that's commitment!

> 'In the beginning, I needed to prove myself to the industry. Not any more. I'm doing this for fun.'
> – Celine Dion

From Eurovision star to Grammy winner!

Thanks a million

In the UK, Celine has had two UK number 1 singles, and both have sold over a million records: 'Think Twice' and 'My Heart Will Go On'. 'My Heart Will Go On' is not just one of the top 10 biggest selling singles of all time - it also won every award going: Grammys, an Oscar, a Golden Globe – you name it!

Horseplay

In 2013, Celine revealed to Jonathan Ross that she went into the Eurovision Song Contest feeling like a horse, because her husband had bet so much money on her to win, and she felt she had to win the race. 'I looked like a horse and I felt like a horse,' she joked. Wonder how much money her husband won when she galloped home in first place?

Full name: Celine Marie Claudette Dion

ESC song: 'Ne partez pas sans moi' ('Don't Leave Without Me')

Score: 137

Age during ESC: 20

Signature look: A white tuxedo with a ballet tutu

Motto: 'I'm not trying to be a nice girl, but it's me. I'm not afraid to be nice.'

Celine won Eurovision by one nail-biting point.

Celine's first record deal was secured when she was twelve and she sang for the Pope at sixteen.

Celine is the youngest of 14 children and she toured with them as part of showbiz troupe Dion's Family.

Grab a Grammy

EUROVISION

There could be an entire library dedicated to number-crunching Eurovision. Here are two pages for starters.

14
The number of times Ukraine has qualified consecutively, between 2003 and 2023. That's more than any other country.

8
The number of times in a row the Netherlands failed to qualify, from 2005 to 2012.

95
The age of the oldest contestant, Emil Ramsauer, who was a member of the 2013 Swiss entry Takasa.

0
The number of points Andorra has scored over their six entries.

11
The age of the youngest contestant, Nathalie Pâque, the French entry for 1989.

5 minutes and 9 seconds
The length of the longest song: 'Corde Della Mia Chitarra' by Nunzio Gallo, for Italy in 1957.

52
The number of countries that have entered the contest.

IN NUMBERS

53 The number of years Portugal had to wait for their first win.

27 The number of countries who have won Eurovision.

68 The number of times Germany has participated in the Eurovision Song Contest.

43 The highest number of competitors seen in a single year (in 2008, 2011 and 2018). The maximum allowed is 44.

1 Morocco has entered once, in 1980.

13 The age of the youngest ever winner, Sandra Kim.

11 The number of times Norway has come last. More than any other country.

138 The number of times Massiel sings 'la' in Spain's 1968 winning song 'La, La, La'.

2 years and 4 days The length of Duncan Laurence's reign as winner – the longest ever because of the COVID cancellation of 2020.

10 top 5 hits for UK entries

1961	The Allisons	Are You Sure?	No 2
1969	Lulu	Boom Bang-a-Bang	No 2
1970	Mary Hopkin	Knock, Knock, Who's There?	No 2
1971	Clodagh Rodgers	Jack in the Box	No 4
1972	The New Seekers	Beg, Steal or Borrow	No 2
1973	Cliff Richard	Power to All Our Friends	No 4
1982	Bardo	One Step Further	No 2
1997	Katrina and the Waves	Love Shine a Light	No 3
2007	Scooch	Flying the Flag (For You)	No 5
2022	Sam Ryder	Space Man	No 2

WE HEART

Eurovision UK number 1s

Nine Eurovision songs have been number 1 in the UK, seven from winners, and two from songs that probably should've won

1967	Sandie Shaw	Puppet On a String (UK)
1968	Cliff Richard	Congratulations (UK: 2nd place)
1970	Dana	All Kinds of Everything (Ireland)
1974	ABBA	Waterloo (Sweden)
1976	Brotherhood of Man	Save Your Kisses For Me (UK)
1980	Johnny Logan	What's Another Year? (Ireland)
1981	Bucks Fizz	Making Your Mind Up (UK)
1982	Nicole	Ein Bißchen Frieden (Germany)
1996	Gina G	Ooh Aah . . . Just A Little Bit (UK: 8th place)

Top 10 most streamed Eurovision songs on Spotify*

1	Duncan Laurence	Arcade	811.3M
2	Måneskin	Zitti e Buoni	343.8M
3	Rosa Linn	Snap	219.7M
4	Alexander Rybak	Fairytale	218.1M
5	Mahmood	Soldi	208.9M
6	ABBA	Waterloo	203.1M
7	Loreen	Euphoria	198.2M
8	Måns Zelmerlöw	Heroes	143.1M
9	Daði & Gagnamagnið	Think About Things	121.2M
10	Mahmood and Blanco	Brividi	113.8M

*as of 9 October 2022

CHARTS

Eurovision is a career launchpad. You don't always have to win on the night to score big. Here's how well some songs performed after the contest.

20 non-UK faves who made the UK top 40

1958	Domenico Modugno	Volare	No 10 (Italy)
1964	Gigliola Cinquetti	Non Ho L'età	No 17 (Italy)
1972	Vicky Leandros	Après Toi	No 2 (Luxembourg)
1975	Teach-In	Ding a Dong	No 13 (Netherlands)
1979	Milk and Honey	Hallelujah	No 5 (Israel)
1987	Johnny Logan	Hold Me Now	No 2 (Ireland)
1998	Dana International	Diva	No 11 (Israel)
2006	Lordi	Hard Rock Hallelujah	No 25 (Finland)
2007	Verka Serduchka	Dancing Lasha Tumbai	No 28 (Ukraine)
2009	Alexander Rybak	Fairytale	No 10 (Norway)
2010	Lena	Satellite	No 30 (Germany)
2012	Loreen	Euphoria	No 3 (Sweden)
2013	Emmelie de Forest	Only Teardrops	No 15 (Denmark)
2014	The Common Linnets	Calm After the Storm	No 9 (Netherlands)
2014	Conchita Wurst	Rise Like a Phoenix	No 17 (Austria)
2015	Måns Zelmerlöw	Heroes	No 11 (Sweden)
2019	Duncan Laurence	Arcade	No 29 (Netherlands)
2020	Daði & Gagnamagnið	Think About Things	No 34 (Iceland)
2021	Måneskin	Zitti e Buoni	No 17 (Italy)
2022	Kalush Orchestra	Stefania	No 38 (Ukraine)

STORY OF A WINNING SONG:
'ARCADE'
BY DUNCAN LAURENCE

2019 was a strong year, but 'Arcade' hit the jackpot for the Netherlands.

If you think 'Arcade' has an emotional power, you'd be right. The song came out of a very dark time, and you can hear that in the lyrics, the music and the passionate vocal delivery. The story behind the song comes from a family friend of Duncan's who suffered the loss of a loved one, and never had the chance to say goodbye.

Time Tiks on

'Arcade' was the addictive song that just wouldn't go away. In 2021, momentum for the song started to build on Tik Tok and videos with #ArcadeDuncanLaurence had 71 million views, whilst videos with #duncanlaurence have had a yikes-inducing 300+ million views.

'Arcade' was co-written by Duncan.

'Arcade' was the first winner for the Netherlands in 44 years. Their last win was Teach-In's 1975 ditty 'Ding-a-Dong'.

'I got bullied a lot when I was younger. And every time I came home from school, music was the thing that helped me cope.' – Duncan Laurence

Winner of winners

'Arcade' isn't just a Eurovision winner, it's the most streamed Eurovision winner ever, by a lot! Not only has the 'small town boy' conquered Spotify, (turn back a page), but in April 2022, the Official Charts Company revealed that his song had had the most plays across all platforms, beating ABBA, Loreen and Måneskin.

Total points: 498 [televote: 261, jury: 237]
Number of douze points awarded: 8
Performance position: 12th
UK chart position: 29th

Enter FLETCHER

'Arcade' was given a new lease of life when Duncan re-recorded the song with fellow LGBTQ+ artist FLETCHER. Their voices blend so well together that once you hear it, it's hard to remember the Eurovision original.

In 2022, Kelly Clarkson performed her own version of 'Arcade'. When Duncan saw it, he said, 'I have no words. Kelly Clarkson, you are a singing goddess.'

'Arcade' has been certified gold in 11 regions, including America, where it has racked up half a million sales.

49

COUNTRY ROADS:

SVERIGE (SWEDEN)

Sweden could win every year, and no one would complain.
They're consistently that good.

1958
ALICE BABS

Sweden entered the contest in its third year with a decent showing, coming fourth with 'Lilla Stjärna' by Alice Babs.

1959
MELODIFESTIVALEN

Every Swedish entry since 1959 has been selected via the national Melodifestivalen competition.

1963
LAST AND LEAST

Monica Zetterlund was the first Swede to bring home the cursed nil-points.

1971-1972
FAMILY FOUR

Squint, and you could mistake the vocal harmony group who represented Sweden two years in a row for ABBA. Did they pave the way for the future winners?

1974
ABBA

Sweden's first ever win was with 'Waterloo' by ABBA, a rare English language song from the country. They had to wait 15 years for this victory.

1984
HERREYS

'Diggi-Loo Diggi-Ley' opened the contest and won. The bouncy nonsensical pop song is as famous for the golden boots worn by the trio of brothers as it is for the song itself.

1991
CAROLA

Singer Carola was the last Swedish winner to win with a song in the national language, 'Fångad av en Stormvind'. Carola had already come third in the contest in 1983 with her song 'Främling'.

1999
CHARLOTTE NILSSON

When 'Take Me to Your Heaven', a song sung in English, won the contest, it ended 22 consecutive years of Swedish language entries and began a 24-year-run of songs in English (one with added French operatics: 'La Voix').

2011
ERIC SAADE

Despite coming first in the semi-final, heartthrob Eric Saade's 'Popular' wasn't popular enough to win. In 2021, Eric entered Melodifestivalen but was pipped at the post with his song 'Every Minute'.

2012
LOREEN

A decade after its win, 'Euphoria' is still seen by plenty of Eurovision fans as the best winner ever. They may have a point, or rather, 12 of them.

2015
MÅNS ZELMERLÖW

'We are the heroes of our time' is an anthemic chorus crafted to bring Eurovision fans to their feet. Sweden's sixth and last winning song was a hit all over Europe, even making it to number 11 in the UK chart.

Ireland has won the contest seven times, but how many of those songs can you hum? They certainly aren't up to 'Waterloo' levels of fame!

Since Eric Saade in 2011, Sweden have finished in the top five a total of eight times.

2022
CORNELIA JAKOBS

She may have only come fourth with 'Hold Me Closer', but Cornelia scored the most points of any Swedish entry ever: a whopping 438.

THEY ARE THE HEROES OF OUR TIME . . .

Conchita Wurst

Like the phoenix itself, Conchita Wurst is a mythical creation, the invention of singer–artist Tom Neuwirth.

If ever a song sounded like a lost Bond theme it's 'Rise Like a Phoenix'.

Three years before The Greatest Showman gave us a fabulous bearded lady with a fabulous song 'This Is Me,' Conchita Wurst had already, been there, done that, got the trophy. With stars like Danny Beard on *Drag Race UK* in 2022, it's easy to forget how unprepared people were for Conchita. Today, glamorous bearded folk seem almost ordinary, but when Tom Neuwirth took to the stage as Conchita in Copenhagen, no one was used to seeing a female-presenting artist who was also unshaven. It was shocking and thought-provoking, and that's before you heard her beautiful voice.

The absolute WURST

No artist wants to repeat what they've done already over and over again, so Tom has said that he will divide his artistic output into two personas, the feminine Conchita and the more masculine-leaning WURST. He released his first album as WURST, Truth Over Magnitude, in 2019.

'The bearded lady is my own truth and a way of expressing myself. Everybody should feel like that. Everybody should create their life however they want.' – Tom Neuwirth

That's What I Am

As is true for so many Eurovision icons, it took Conchita a couple of goes before she made it to the contest. In 2012, Conchita entered Austria's selection show, *Austria Rocks the Contest*, with an empowering power ballad called 'That's What I Am'. Conchita very nearly was the Austrian 2012 entry, but she eventually came second with 49% of the vote.

Full name: Conchita Wurst

ESC song: 'Rise Like a Phoenix'

Score: 290

Age during ESC: 25

Signature look: Slinky dress, jet black hair and a lustrous beard to match

Motto: 'I have never promised to anyone that I am a role model,' or that I am perfect. I am simply me, one person, a human being.' Tom Neuwirth

For a short time, Tom was in a boy band called Jetzt Anders!

Queen of drag

Conchita is the drag persona of Tom Neuwirth. Tom identifies as male and uses the pronouns he/him when not performing as Conchita. Conchita made her first appearance on a TV talent show in Austria in 2011 called *Die Große Chance*. She came sixth. By 2019, Conchita was co-hosting her own star-search show: Austria's answer to *RuPaul's Drag Race*, *Queen of Drags* with Heidi Klum.

The endless rebirth of Conchita

In a 2022 interview, Tom/Conchita said, 'Once you are a member of the Eurovision family, they never let you go,' and that's very true. Conchita returned to Eurovision to perform in 2015 as all winners do, and then popped back again in 2019 as part of the 'Switch Song' routine that saw her sing 'Heroes' by Måns Zelmerlöw.

STORY OF A WINNING SONG:
'EUPHORIA'
BY LOREEN

The banging-est banger that ever was signalled a new era for Eurovision: one where the songs could be radio hits again.

Loreen's win in 2012 was a breath of fresh air, and it wasn't just the wind machine in her hair. 'Euphoria' was a song that some might say was 'too good' for Eurovision, a song that anyone from Sia to Beyoncé would've jumped at having.

Loreen was so far ahead of the witchy trend, that people forget she was doing it years before it caught on. It's only a matter of time until TikTok subgroup WitchTok discovers Loreen and a new generation finds 'Euphoria'.

What a Douzey

Here's a list of every country that gave Loreen the maximum 12 points – the most ever received up to that point: Austria, Belgium, Denmark, Estonia, Finland, France, Germany, Hungary, Iceland, Ireland, Israel, Latvia, Netherlands, Norway, Russia, Slovakia, Spain, and the UK.

'I knew that it was going to be completely different. And when things are different, people get afraid, but I went on following my intuition.'
– Loreen.

High contrast art

Sweden is great at producing music that combines opposing forces. Much of ABBA's success is based on a happy-sad disco formula. Loreen's Eurovision performance of 'Euphoria' does something similar, taking a polished club track and making it primal. With dark and dramatic staging, it provided all the drama that Eurovision fans love.

Total points: 372
Number of douze points awarded: 18
Performance position: 17th
UK chart: 3rd

What do you mean I won?

When Loreen won, she didn't realise she'd won. In fact, she was the last person to twig. 'I didn't get that I had won,' she told Steve Holden in an interview for the official Eurovision podcast. 'I thought the 12 points were basically a jury and then after that people had to vote.' So, when her producer told her to go back on stage to perform the song again, she was totally unprepared, saying, 'Wait, I have to do some meditation.' Which, by the way, is the perfect response to anyone asking you do something.

Fan favourite 4eva

Every year fans vote for their favourite Eurovision track at Songfestival.be. 'Euphoria' has come first 10 out of 13 times!

No compromise

Some artists are hardcore Eurovision fans. Not Loreen, she didn't know much about Eurovision and that gave her the creative freedom to do what she wanted. When she planned her bewitching performance with no fancy clothes, no shoes, and barely any light it felt dangerous. 'It was just such an awakening moment,' she said.

An everlasting piece of art

The only country not to award 'Euphoria' any points was Italy. What was their problem?

DOUZE FACTS

You can never have enough love, sleep and Eurovision facts.

1
Poor Portugal and Lithuania are the only two countries that scored nil-points on their debut appearances at the contest – what a kick in the teeth.

2
1987 was the last year that the scoreboard was operated manually; from 1988 it was computer operated.

3
Israel was the first non-European country to join Eurovision in 1973.

4
Every year Eurovision has a slogan and theme. Some of the best are: Share the Moment (2010), Celebrate Diversity (2017) and Open Up (2021).

5
Despite only winning five times, the UK has hosted the contest nine times, including 2023.

6
In 2017, Ukranian joker Vitalii Sediuk stormed the stage during Jamala's performance of 'I Believe in U' and mooned (flashed his bum) draped in an Australian flag. He was fined €284.

7

Hazell Dean, a bona fide pop star, entered the UK's Song for Europe contest twice and lost out both times. She finally made it to the Grand Final main stage singing back-up vocals for Samantha Janus in 1991.

8

The first time the competition had an all-male top five was in 2019. There was an all-female top five in 2002.

9

Lordi broke the world karaoke record in 2006 when 80,000 people sang Lordi's 'Hard Rock Hallelujah' in Helskini.

10

When Celine Dion won Eurovision with 'Ne partez pas sans moi' in 1988, it was the last time a French language song won.

11

In 2011, Azerbaijan won the contest with their song 'Running Scared', but weirdly they didn't get enough votes to win their semi-final heat: Greece did.

12

When Lynsey de Paul and Mike Moran came second in 1977 with 'Rock Bottom', they were the first British contestants to write their own song.

DOING THE MOST & LEAST

You wanted drama; here's the contest with the most.

Longest wait for a win

52 years for Malta. They joined in 1971, but Malta have still never won. Cyprus joined in 1981, 42 years ago, and they're still waiting too. Should have been 'Fuego' – sorry, said it.

Longest wait for a win after winning

53 years. Spain won in 1968 and tied in 1969, but have never won again.

Top 5 host cities:

Dublin: 6
London: 4
Luxembourg: 4
Copenhagen: 3
Stockholm: 3

Most consecutive top 10s

20! The UK made every top 10 between 1957 and 1977.

Biggest points drop

Portugal have lost the most points between contests, going from 758 in 2017 to coming last in 2018 with 39.

Top 5 host countries

UK: 9
Ireland: 7
Sweden: 6
Netherlands: 5
Luxembourg: 4

Least qualifying

North Macedonia – only once since 2009.

Semi-winners only

The following countries all won a semi-final but have never actually won: Iceland in 2009, Australia in 2016 and 2019, and Bulgaria in 2017. Gutting.

Top five winning languages

1. English: 31 wins
2. French: 14 wins
3. Dutch: Hebrew, Italian: 3 wins

Failed to make the top 10

Since winning in 2006, Finland has failed to make the top 10.

Top five most frequent winners

1. Ireland: 7 wins
2. Sweden: 6 wins
3. France, Luxembourg, The Netherlands, UK: 5 wins
4. Israel: 4 wins
5. Denmark, Italy, Norway, Ukraine: 3 wins

Most semi-finals won

Two! Alexander Rybak won both semi-finals that he entered.

Longest participation streak

UK – 63 contests in a row.

Viewer Facts and Fan-fiction

How much do we love Eurovision? This much ...

161 million people watched the 2022 Eurovision Song Contest! And that was down on the previous year's 183 million viewers because of Russia's exclusion. UK audience figures were the highest of any country. Between 8.9 million and 10.6 million people watched the Grand Final in 2022, the highest audience figure for a decade. Perhaps the fact Sam Ryder's 'Space Man' had so much buzz made Brits tune in. The viewing share of the Grand Final – that's the percentage of people watching TV choosing Eurovision – was 43.3%, but for viewers aged fifteen to twenty-four, it was 56.2%, meaning the contest is getting younger viewers more excited than ever. #BlameMåneskin♥

TikTok takes off

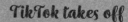

TikTok became an official partner in 2022 and livestreamed all three live shows – making access to Eurovision possible for anyone in the world with a phone. 3.3 million people watched the live Grand Final on TikTok and 7.6 million people watched it on YouTube. The most views (2.2 million) came from Ukraine, the winning country.

FAN-TASY WINNERS

How might the ESC winners' circle look if fans like you were voting?

The Organisation Generale des Amateurs de L'Eurovision (OGAE), is the largest independent Eurovision fan club, with over 10,000 members from 50+ countries. Each year its members vote for their winning song before the contest takes place. Sometimes they get it right, and sometimes . . . well, they don't.

Here's how they've voted over the last 10 years.

OGAE'S WINNERS

Year	OGAE winner	Artist	Country	Actual placing
2012	Euphoria	Loreen	Sweden	1
2013	Only Teardrops	Emmelie de Forest	Denmark	1
2014	Undo	Sanna Nielsen	Sweden	3
2015	Grande Amore	Il Volo	Italy	3
2016	J'ai cherché	Amir	France	6
2017	Occidentali's Karma	Francesco Gabbani	Italy	6
2018	Toy	Netta	Israel	1
2019	Soldi	Mahmood	Italy	2
2020	On Fire	The Roop	Lithuania	N/A
2021	Je me casse	Destiny	Malta	7
2022	Hold Me Closer	Cornelia Jakobs	Sweden	4

SECOND BEST

When Sam Ryder came second in 2022, he was following in a long, long, long line of UK contestants that were pipped at the post.

The UK has come second more than any other country. Why are they runners-up so often? Maybe their songs aren't the best, but so far there have been 16 songs that were very nearly winners. Which do you think were most robbed?

1959: Pearl Carr and Teddy Johnson – Sing, Little Birdie

1960: Bryan Johnson – Looking High, High, High

1961: The Allisons – Are You Sure?

1964: Matt Monro – I Love the Little Things

1965: Kathy Kirby – I Belong

1968: Cliff Richard – Congratulations

1970: Mary Hopkin – Knock, Knock, Who's There?

1972: The New Seekers – Beg, Steal or Borrow

1975 : The Shadows – Let Me Be the One

1977: Lynsey de Paul and Mike Moran – Rock Bottom

1988: Scott Fitzgerald – Go

1989: Live Report – Why Do I Always Get It Wrong?

1992: Michael Ball – One Step Out of Time

1993: Sonia – Better the Devil You Know

1998: Imaani – Where Are You?

2022: Sam Ryder – Space Man

Lynsey de Paul came second with the first ever self-penned song by a British performer

BACK FOR SECONDS

Should artists go for the double and come back to the contest?

Some performers love Eurovision so much that they can't wait to do it again, but while some come back and triumph, others virtually undo their legacy with an underwhelming showing. When that happens, we do the most polite thing we can: pretend it didn't happen.

Third time's a charm for Sergey Lazarev

Artist	First song	Score	Second song	Score	Good idea?
Alexander Rybak	Fairytale	1st	That's How You Write a Song	15th	No
Anne-Marie David	Tu te reconnaîtras	1st	Je suis l'enfant soleil	3rd	Yes
Cliff Richard	Congratulations	2nd	Power to All Our Friends	3rd	Yes
Charlotte Perrelli	Take Me to Your Heaven	1st	Hero	18th	No
Dana International	Diva	1st	Ding Dong	FTQ	No
Dima Bilan	Never Let You Go	2nd	Believe	1st	Yes
Helena Paparizou	Die For You	3rd	My Number One	1st	Yes
Johnny Logan	What's Another Year?	1st	Hold Me Now	1st	Yes
Linda Martin	Terminal 3	2nd	Why Me?	1st	Yes
Lena	Satellite	1st	Taken by a Stranger	10th	No
Mahmood	Soldi	2nd	Brividi	6th	Yes
Natalia Gordienko	Loca	20th	Sugar	13th	Yes
Niamh Kavanagh	In Your Eyes	1st	It's For You	23rd	No
Poli Genova	Na Inat	FTQ	If Love Was a Crime	4th	Yes
Sakis Rouvas	Shake It	3rd	This is Our Night	7th	Yes
Sergey Lazarev	You Are the Only One	3rd	Scream	3rd	Yes
Sunstroke Project	Run Away	10th	Hey Mamma	3rd	Yes

FTQ = Failed to qualify at semi-finals

COUNTRY ROADS: UKRAYNA (UKRAINE)

Ukraine play to win, no joke. Nearly every song they enter could be a worthy winner.

2003
Late arrivals
Ukraine arrived late to the continental party with their first ever song 'Hasta La Vista', a weird Spanish/English hybrid by Oleksandr Ponomariov. It didn't do great.

2004
Ruslana
Fast learners, Ukraine realised that something more authentic might resonate better, and the powerful dance/rock track 'Wild Dances' by Ruslana, complete with fierce choreography and traditional instruments, won.

2005
Ukraine hosted the contest for the first time in the capital Kyiv. The slogan for the year was Awakening.

The only countries with more top five placing songs in the twenty-first century are Sweden and Russia.

2007
Verka Serduchka
Why Ukraine sent a song sung in German by a drag queen with the subtitle 'lasha tumbai' (which is supposedly Mongolian for 'whipped cream'), we may never know. But we're glad they did. 'Dancing Lasha Tumbai' should've won (it came 2nd), there, I said it.

Pink bucket hat icons Kalush Orchestra

2008
Ani Lorak

After coming so close to winning with Verka, Ukraine sent another total classic bop, 'Shady Lady' with an incredible performance by Ani Lorak. It came second, again!

2014
Hamster Wheel

When Mariya Yaremchuk entered with pop banger 'Tick Tock', it sounded like a big hit. But the staging choice of a man in a giant hamster wheel is the iconic part that sealed the song in history.

2016
Jamala

Eurovision is not supposed to be political, but the song 1944 by Jamala about the deportation of Crimean Tatars (the indigenous people of Crimea) by Soviet leader Joseph Stalin was pretty political. The song and its message connected with audiences and Ukraine secured their second win.

2017
Host year/worst year

The second time Ukraine hosted the contest, they did the worst they ever have, coming 24th with the song 'Time' by O. Torvald.

2021
Go_A

'Shum' by Go_A: What a song. A beast of an electro club track with traditional folk elements and a unique powerful vocal by Kateryna Pavlenko. It came second in its semi-final, but ultimately only placed fifth in the Grand Final.

Ukraine is the only country to qualify for every ESC they have competed in since 2004.

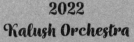

2022
Kalush Orchestra

When Kalush Orchestra won in 2022, of course audience sentiments were with the country that had just been invaded by Russia, and it scored the highest audience vote in history, 439 points from the public alone. But it wasn't just a gesture; Eurovision's first winning rap song was a touching ode to mothers and everything they do for us #Kalush_Family.

Hard worker Verka

THEY ARE THE HEROES OF OUR TIME . . .

Daði & Gagnamagnið

Daði Freyr with his rag-tag band of mates and family is the lost Eurovision winner – sorry, Cliff Richard, we've moved on.

Eurovision's Lost Winner

Even though Eurovision 2020 was cancelled due to COVID, Daði Freyr and 'Think About Things' became an almost overnight sensation, going viral and racking up millions of streams. In 2022, the Official Charts Company revealed the most streamed Eurovision songs of all time, and 'Think About Things' was at number 3. It didn't even compete in the contest but still managed to rack up the plays.

Daði Freyr is like a mythical Eurovision creature – he's rarely seen, yet he's extremely tall, 6ft 9, and impossible to miss. Daði is one of the most popular acts to ever be involved at Eurovision, with two massive hit songs in back-to-back years! His position in Eurovision history will be debated till the end of time. Would he have won the 2020 contest if it had gone ahead?

'Because you can have six people on stage, I decided of course I'm going to bring as many people as I can, because it's gonna be more fun.' – Daði Freyr

Fam-tastic

Daði keeps his friends close and his family just as close. Not only is his band, Gagnamagnið, made up of some of his best mates, his wife, Árný, and sister, Sigrún, are also along for the fun. It's no surprise the siblings are musical; their dad Pétur was a musician and even tried out for Eurovision in 1993. Sadly, his band came ninth in the national selection show.

ESC song: 10 Years

Total points: 1378

Age during ESC: 28

Signature look: Turqoise sweatshirt with pixel art versions of each band member's face on them

Motto: 'Eurovision is an incredible opportunity to do crazy stuff that you wouldn't be able to do unless you're Lady Gaga or Beyoncé.' Daði Freyr

Band line-up: Daði Freyr Pétursson, Árný Fjóla Ásmundsdóttir, Hulda Kristín Kolbrúnardóttir, Jóhann Sigurður Jóhannsson, Sigrún Birna Pétursdóttir, Stefán Hannesson

Daði is pronounced somewhere between 'dathi' and 'dah-dee'.

The band serving matchy-matchy, down-to-earth DIY

'10 Years' was written about Daði's 10 year first kiss anniversary with his wife.

Fourth of nature

After the massive success of 'Think About Things', Daði & Gagnamagnið already had a huge task on their hands – to follow it up in 2021. Then COVID struck AGAIN and scuppered their chances in a new and excruciating way. One member of the band tested positive for COVID-19 and they were unable to perform live at the show, with footage of their rehearsal being shown instead. Even with that setback, the song came 4th in the final.

No sweat-er

At Eurovision, you can't actually plug your instruments in, so as an act of artistic rebellion (a very cute one) Daði decided to invent instruments out of old PlayStation controllers and plastic gizmos with buttons on, for the band to mime with. That old-fashioned computer aesthetic became a literal motif that they sewed on to their iconic matching turquoise sweatshirts.

PARLEZ-VOUS

How do you entertain dozens of countries when they don't speak your language? Keep repeating words over and over again, that's how.

Irritating scale

1 Catchy
2 Earworm
3 Patience testing
4 Beyond a joke
5 Turn it off!

1959
Jean Philippe went 'Oui, Oui, Oui, Oui' all the way home (3rd).
Irritating rating: 2

1962
If you think 'Baby Shark' is annoying, give 'Ring-a-Ding Girl' by Ronnie Carroll a listen.
Irritating rating: 4

1967
Thérèse Steinmetz's shameless rip-off, 'Ring-Dinge-Ding' for the Netherlands is even worse.
Irritating rating: 5

1968
Spain's 'La, La, La' isn't bad, they just forgot to write a chorus.
Irritating rating: 3

1969
'Boom Bang-a-Bang' by Lulu didn't start the kiddie-talk sing-songs, but she cemented their stay with her win.
Irritating rating: 2

1973
Marion Rung from Finland had a lot of fun with 'Tom Tom Tom' – us, less so.
Irritating rating: 3

1975
ABBA were no stranger to silly song titles, so after they won, Teach-In thought 'in for a pfennig' and actually won with (ding) 'Ding a Dong'.
Irritating rating: 1

68

GIBBERISH?

1976
Switzerland's song about a clown called, 'Djambo, Djambo', was just an excuse to repeat the words djambo, djambo.
Irritating rating: 3

1976
'Sing Sang Song' by Germany's Les Humphries Singers is pretty unbelievable. It makes the *RuPaul's Drag Race* song, 'Bing Bang Bong' seem like a Beyoncé hit.
Irritating rating: 5

1977
With 'Boom Boom Boomerang', Austria lost their minds. The performance is a literal *Saturday Night Live* sketch.
Irritating rating: 5

1980
'Papa Pingouin' has a lot of p-p-ps, and should be wretched listening, but somehow twins Sophie and Magaly, for Luxembourg, p-p-p-pulled it off.
Irritating rating: 2

1984
'Diggi-Loo Diggi-Ley' by Herreys is babble-pop at its best. No notes! No bum ones anyway.
Irritating rating: 1

1985
Turkey's 'Didai Didai Dai' is one step away from having a chorus that goes di-dum-di-dum, dum. Catchy, though.
Irritating rating: 3

2006
'There is a way to understand without a language.' So sang Treble in the song 'Amambanda', which featured more gobbledygook than any song before or since.
Irritating rating: 4

2019
'Say Na Na Na' by singing dentist Serhat is a certified sad banger. It's like San Marino were saying 'this is how you do meaningless chorus'.
Irritating rating: 1

2008
'Baila el Chiki Chiki' was a joke song by a joke entrant, Rodolpho Chikilicuatre, who had a quiffy wig and a tiny plastic guitar. Guess Spain really didn't want to win.
Irritating rating: 5

NEIGHBOUR

ICELAND · NORWAY · SWEDEN · FINLAND · RUSSIA · ESTONIA · LATVIA · LITHUANIA · DENMARK · IRELAND · UNITED KINGDOM · NETHERLANDS · BELGIUM · LUXEMBURG · GERMANY · POLAND · BELARUS · UKRAINE · CZECH REPUBLIC · SLOVAKIA · FRANCE · SWITZERLAND · LIECHTENSTEIN · AUSTRIA · HUNGARY · MOLDOVA · ROMANIA · PORTUGAL · SPAIN · ANDORRA · MONACO · SAN MARINO · ITALY · SLOVENIA · CROATIA · BOSNIA AND HERZEGOVINA · SERBIA · BULGARIA · GEORGIA · ARMENIA · AZE... · MONTENEGRO · ALBANIA · MACEDONIA · GREECE · TURKEY · CYPRUS · MOROCCO · MALTA

Eurovision Friend Contest

A Canadian study, published in 2017, surveyed 500+ European Eurovision fans and found that less than a third of respondents (26%) voted for their favourite song. Almost three quarters of people voted for the song they thought would win or gave their support to songs from their preferred countries or performers they identified with because of shared backgrounds, culture or language.

FAVOUR

Regional bloc voting is not just predictable and annoying, it's a bit cringe.

Countries that border each other naturally share tastes and cultural history, so of course they share points too - joking/not joking. In 2021, there were 78 douze points to be handed out: half from the jury, half from the televote. 21 were given to neighbours (that's one in four). In 2019, it was approximately one in three. In a way, we should be pleased that neighbours get along and don't metaphorically throw cat poop over the garden wall.

AUSTRALIA

ISRAEL

The four main voting blocs

The cliques of Europe traditionally break down like this (although friendly alliances come and go, as anyone who watches the news knows).

1 Eastern Europe: Russia, Belarus, Ukraine, Georgia

2 Nordics: Norway, Sweden, Denmark, Finland, the Netherlands, Estonia, Latvia, Lithuania

3 North Balkans: Romania, Moldova, Slovenia, Croatia, Serbia

4 South Balkans: Greece, Cyprus, Albania, Malta, Bulgaria, North Macedonia

Second in the favouritism stakes is Moldova and Romania. Since 2000, the average score Moldova has given to Romania is 10.8.

Greece-y does it

Of the 31 times (1981 to 2022) that Cyprus has been able to vote for Greece in the final, it has given them 12 points 26 times. Greece consistently returns the favour. 'Over the years people say this is ludicrous, but still they do it. They just don't care,' said Terry Wogan back in 2007. Fast forward to 2022, and it's still happening like clockwork.

The UK is not without bias. Ireland is the UK's closest ally, followed by the south-western European countries, Austria, Portugal, Germany, Belgium and France.

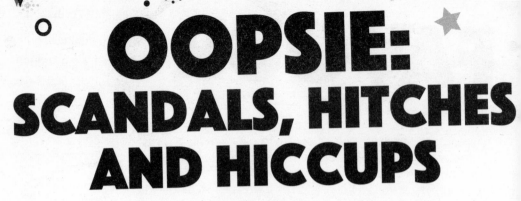

OOPSIE: SCANDALS, HITCHES AND HICCUPS

Eurovision could be described as so wrong it's right, but sometimes it literally does go wrong.

1957
The scandalous 13-second kiss between Denmark's Gustav Winckler and Birthe Wilke apparently only happened because producers failed to say cut.

1962
A power cut nearly put an end to the show, plunging the stage into darkness during the Netherlands' performance.

1981
Italy boycotted the ESC in 1981, saying it was too old-fashioned. Bet they ate their words when they saw Bucks Fizz!

1985
The best wardrobe malfunction surely comes from Swedish presenter Lill Lindfors, who 'accidentally' ripped her skirt off, only to reveal that her shirt transformed into a whole other dress.

1986
Sandra Kim won Eurovision when she was only thirteen, although her song lyrics said she was fifteen.

1987
Lotta Engberg from Sweden's song, 'Fyra Bugg Och En Coca-Cola' had to be resubmitted without reference to the soft drink brand. The song was renamed 'Boogaloo'.

1999

Israeli winner Dana International didn't realise how heavy the award she would be presenting was when she returned the following year and toppled over when it was handed to her.

2001

In 2001, Soren Pilmark, the Danish presenter, dropped and smashed the trophy. Except it was only a gag and the real trophy was fine.

2005

UK entrant Javine Hylton had a wardrobe mishap and revealed a bit of boob. 'Oh, my God, that was so embarrassing,' she said.

2009

Jade Ewen was almost jabbed in the ribs by her own violinist – accidentally, of course.

2013

Carola Häggkvist of Sweden actually fell off the stage. Cringe. Ouch. Oh dear.

2017

Vitalii Sediuk stormed the stage during a performance by 2016's winner, Jamala, and showed his bum, wrapped in an Australian flag – sure . . .

2016

Romania was ejected from Eurovision due to unpaid debts to the European Broadcasting Union.

2021

Natalia Gordienko dropped her microphone but was such a pro,= that she picked it up so quickly almost no one noticed.

2021

Non-stretch fabrics do not stretch, they rip, as Damiano found out after Mäneskin's winning performance, when his leather trousers ripped at the crotch.

2022

Six national juries were removed from the ESC due to irregular voting patterns: Azerbaijan, Georgia, Montenegro, Poland, Romania and San Marino. Tsk.

STORY OF A WINNING SONG:

'FAIRYTALE

BY ALEXANDER RYBAK

Norway's 2009 win was no fairytale for its writer and singer – it happened, it was real and it was massive.

Some say that the way to stand out in Eurovision is to have a gimmick. Well, Alexander Rybak has the best, most recognisable 'gimmick' of any Eurovision winner – his violin. Of course, it's not a gimmick, it's an amazing skill, but it does also make him unforgettable. There's a reason why 10 years after his Eurovision win, he was asked to be in the Eurovision movie – because his image and legacy as a Eurovision icon endure to this day.

All about Alexander

'Fairytale' is a brilliant song, but Alexander really sells it. When he won in 2009, he was only twenty-three, making him the youngest male winner of the contest. If that wasn't impressive enough, 'Fairytale' was also written entirely by Alexander himself, words and music, and of course he played the violin too!

For the 2011 contest, Alexander worked as Norway's roving reporter, interviewing the acts for national broadcaster NRK.

'I love every time I get to perform it. "Fairytale" lets me have fun with music.'
– Alexander Rybak

Fiddle dee dee

Instruments on stage are not actually allowed to be plugged in. You can play them, but nobody will hear them. At first this worried Alexander, but his energetic performance was made possible by the fact that he didn't have to play his violin perfectly. He could concentrate on his vocals and put on a jaw-dropping show 'playing' the violin in a way no musician in a real life could.

Alexander is Norwegian, but he was born in Minsk in Belarus. His father, Igor Rybak, was a professional violinist who defected to Norway in the early nineties.

Chart-breaking

Not all Eurovision winning songs are hits. The contest is entertainment Marmite (or should that be herring?), turning off as many people as it delights. Well, 'Fairytale' delighted a lot of people, and after the contest, the single went to number 1 in Belgium, Denmark, Finland, Iceland, Norway and Sweden, as well as going top 10 in the UK, Germany, Greece, Switzerland and the Netherlands.

Fairytale: a tale

The song, based on Alexander's real-life experience of longing for a lost love, is totally relatable to anyone who has ever been dumped, and created a make-believe fantasy in their head of being with the person. 'I'm in love with a fairytale, even though it hurts.' We've all been there, sigh.

Record-breaker

When Alexander Rybak won Eurovision, he did so in the most astonishing way, breaking every record as he went. It all started at the Melodi Grand Prix 2009, Norway's selection contest, where 'Fairytale' won the biggest victory in the history of the contest. Then, at Eurovision, he earned 387 points, the most anyone had ever been given. He also won 16 scores of douze points, which was the most ever received at that time.

The 'happily ever after' ending he deserved

Top five findings

1. The songs of Eurovision winners seem to be getting slower. The average BPM (beats per minute) of the top three songs dropped from 148 BPM in 2010 to 76 BPM in 2019.

2. 69% of all songs were love songs. 83% of winners' songs were love songs.

3. 65% of songs were in a minor key, meaning they sound more melancholy.

4. Male and female lead vocals are neck and neck, and far and away the most popular acts, followed by duos and groups.

5. Key changes appeared in 20% of songs, but not in any of the winning songs.

BANGERS

Which does better, a sob-a-thon slowie or a triumphant toe-tapper?

Forget east vs west voting patterns, the real battle every Eurovision is the one between the emotional songs that capture your heart and energetic bops that get you dancing. Luckily enough, in 2020, two musicologists, Professor Joe Bennett and Simon Troup, looked at the content of 259 finalist songs (from 2009–2019) to see what type of songs did better than others. This is what they found.

Scores for 2020

2020 was cancelled, but musicologist Bennet applied what he'd learned from previous year's shows and scored some of the songs accordingly.

Latvia, Samanta Tina, 'Still Breathing', 0 points

Georgia, Tornike Kipiani, 'Take Me As I Am', 3 points

Denmark, Ben & Tan, 'Yes', 4 points

UK, James Newman, 'My Last Breath', 5 points

Ireland, Lesley Roy, 'Story of My Life', 8 Points

Iceland, Daði Freyr, 'Think About Things', 12 points

Popularity of seven styles of song

27% Eurovision-pop – Upbeat electropop or dance number, e.g. Chanel's 'SloMo'.

22% anthem – Mid-tempo pop song with a big chorus, e.g. Sam Ryder's 'Space Man'.

20% ballad – Slow song that builds to a crashing crescendo, e.g. Gjon's Tears 'Tout l'univers'.

16% niche – Any atypical genre like rock, rap or reggaeton, e.g. Måneskin's 'Zitti e Buoni'.

10% ethno-pop – Combo of chart pop and traditional sounds, e.g. Efendi's 'Cleopatra'.

4% schlager – A sentimental sing-song with an oompah beat, e.g. DoReDoS' 'My Lucky Day'.

1% chanson – Stripped-back French-inspired ballad, e.g. Barbara Pravi's 'Voilà'.

VS BALLADS

CONCLUSION

Slower love songs win . . .
until they bore the audience
and don't.

77

COUNTRY ROADS: LA FRANCE (FRANCE)

France started strong but has struggled to find its place in the modern contest.

1956
Premier in
In the beginning, there was France. France was not only present at the first ever Eurovision, or Grand Prix Eurovision de la Chanson Européenne as it was known then, but seven of the songs at the first contest were sung in French!

1958–1962
André Claveau
France was one of the first powerhouse countries of Eurovision, winning in 1958, 1960 and 1962. André Claveau won first with 'Dors, mon amour', then Jacqueline Boyer took the trophy with 'Tom Pilibi', then two years later Isabelle Aubret's 'Un premier amour' won.

Jacqueline Boyer, a star of France's early heyday

1969
Frida Boccara
One of the four-way winners, Moroccan-born Frida won alongside the likes of the UK's Lulu with a sentimental ballad, 'un jour, en Enfant'.

1974 Pompidou's passing
France's entry Dani withdrew from the contest after the death of the president Georges Pompidou. A shame, because 'La vie a vingt-cinq ans' is rousing French schlager that might've done well.

1977
Marie Myriam

'L'oiseau et L'enfant' which translates to 'the bird and the child', was a decent sing-along, but already sounded pretty dated when it won.

1978-1981
Three threes

Over the course of four Eurovisions, France came third three times. 1979's 'Je suis L'enfant soliel', was yet another song with the calculatedly evocative word 'child' in the title. 1981's idealistic 'Humanahum' by Jean Gabilou was better.

2001
Natasha St-Pier

'Je n'ai que mon âme' was sung by a Canadian singer who sounded very much like another Canadian singer who'd won Eurovision 13 years before: Celine Dion. Natasha came 4th.

2009
Patricia Kaas

When Patricia entered the ESC in 2009, she was already an established star and a favourite to win with her classic chanson song 'Et s'il fallait le faire'. Surprisingly, she only came 8th. Fans of 'Voilà' by Barbara Pravi should check it out.

2014
Dernier position

Twin Twin's 'Moustache' was the first and last time France came last. The catchy rap track scored two measly points: one from Sweden, one from Finland.

2016
Amir

Fan favourite Amir's 'J'ai cherché' could've been France's first win in decades. The music video has well over 100 million views on YouTube, about the same as the 2016 top three videos combined.

France is the only country of the Big Five never to have received nil-points.

2021
Barbara Pravi

If you struggle to understand what people mean when they describe a song as being in the genre of 'chanson', listen to the impassioned ballad 'Voilà' by Barbara Pravi: France's best performing entry since 1991, with 499 points.

Many of the French-language winners we know from Eurovision are actually entries from other countries, such as Luxembourg, Belgium and Switzerland.

Forgotten Faves from Semi-finals

Just because they didn't make the Grand Final doesn't mean these 10 Eurovision songs should be slept on.

1 2019, Poland, 'Fire of Love' by Tulia
It was a strong year, but this unique doom-pop offering was one of the best songs of the contest. The vocal harmonising girl group missed the final by two points. Argh!!!

2 2016, Iceland, 'Hear Them Calling' by Greta Salóme
How was this not in the final? An urgent dramatic Eurovision classic with compelling staging – #robbed.

3 2006, Belgium, 'Je t'adore' by Kate Ryan
This noughties pop tune had hit written all over it, but maybe it was too good or not cheesy enough, or was too much of a Rachel Stevens-sounding throwback.

4 2017, Finland, 'Blackbird' by Norma John
Did Adele enter Eurovision? No, she didn't, but you could be fooled when you hear this ballad.

5 2018, Switzerland, 'Stones' by ZiBBZ
Rock doesn't always do well, so brother-sister duo ZiBBZ failed to make the final, despite having an utterly memorable and iconic song.

6 2022, Albania, 'Sekret' by Ronela Hajati
The Grand Final of 2022 was not exactly packed with bops, so the addition of this powerful Eastern-influenced floor-filler would've made things totally pop.

7 2010, Sweden, 'This is My Life' by Anna Bergendahl
One of the biggest failures in Swedish Eurovision history is still a nice enough folk ballad.

8 2011, Norway, 'Haba Haba' by Stella Mwangi
Even when you have an uplifting message, catchy song and charismatic singer, you can still fail.

9 2016, Ireland, 'Sunlight' by Nicky Byrne
The Westlife singer deserved better. It's not a winning song, but this drivetime radio-friendly rock-pop entry is very good.

10 2019, Hungary, 'Az én apám' by Joci Pápai
All the elements are there in this low-key anthem dripping with emotion but perhaps Mahmood was too similar.

SOLDI:
THE COST OF EUROVISION

In 2023, three countries pulled out of the contest because the cost was too steep: Bulgaria, North Macedonia and Montenegro.

The greatest week of the year comes at considerable expense.

In 2022, tickets to go to Eurovision ranged from €20 to €350.

Liverpool, 2023

When Eurovision comes to Liverpool in 2023, the BBC is expected to pick up the majority of the cost – estimated to be between £8 and £17 million.

Turin, 2022

The deputy mayor of Turin, Michela Favaro, revealed that after their city held the contest in 2022, the hospitality sector made seven times as much money as Italy had paid to host the event: €10 million!

Rotterdam, 2021

Rotterdam spent €19 million hosting the contest two years after Duncan Laurence's victory. Sadly, because it happened during the COVID pandemic, the Dutch city didn't make much money – only €2.8m.

Most expensive Eurovision

When Azerbaijan hosted the Eurovision in Baku that saw Loreen take the trophy in 2012, it was the most expensive contest ever. £60 million was spent on the show and another whopping £100 million on the arena.

Suggested profits/ losses

Eurovision economics explained: don't overspend, and you'll make a killing.

Malmö, Sweden, 2013
Spent: €14.5 million
Made back: €21.5 million
Loss: €7 million

Copenhagen, Denmark, 2014
Spent: €45 million (they built a brand new venue - EXPENSIVE!)
Made back: €116.7 million
Loss: €28.3 million

Vienna, Austria, 2015
Spent: €37 million
Made back: €29.7 million
Loss: €7.3 million

Stockholm, Sweden, 2016
Spent: €13.5 million
Made back: €37.5 million
Profit: €27 million

THEY ARE THE HEROES
OF OUR TIME . . .
ABBA

ABBA need no introduction, so . . .

When ABBA entered the Eurovision Song Contest, they were an up-and-coming Swedish group formed of two married couples. Not the blueprint you'd expect for international stardom, but ABBA turned out to be not just the greatest Eurovision act of all time, but the biggest pop group in the world. They were the complete package. It's never just about the song, it's the song plus the voice plus presentation plus hitting the mood of the time. Do that, and like ABBA we'll promise to love you forevermore.

Benny and Björn have said that they would consider writing a song for the UK to enter into Eurovision.

'I would tell my younger self that winning the Eurovision Song Contest with "Waterloo" in 1974 will be the most fantastic thing, but it will also bring problems.'
– Agnetha

Waterloo almost wasn't

Can you believe it? 'Waterloo' wasn't going to be the song ABBA submitted for the contest! Instead, they were going to submit 'Hasta Mañana', a sweet, but not massively exciting song. The band choose 'Waterloo' instead because its vocals were evenly split between Frida and Agnetha. Björn later said, 'It could've been "Hasta Mañana", and this would never have happened. It never would've won.'

Second time lucky

'Waterloo' caused such a sensation that imagining ABBA's arrival on the global stage in any other way seems impossible, but ABBA had actually tried and failed to enter Eurovision before they won in Brighton. In 1973, ABBA entered their song 'Ring, Ring' into the selection show Melodifestivalen, but it only came third.

ESC song: 'Waterloo'

Score: 24

Signature look: Shiny shirts, flouncy skirts and flares tucked into silver platform boots.

Motto: "How can there be a formula? If there is a secret, it's trying to be as sincere as possible. Writing something like 'Mamma Mia' or 'Fernando' is not guesswork." Benny

Band members: Anni-Frid Lyngstad, Benny Andersson, Björn Ulvaeus, Agnetha Fältskog

If you ever meet Frida, don't call her Frida, or even Anni-Frid, but Serene Highness. After Frida split up with Benny, she married Prince Heinrich Ruzzo Reuss.

Mamma Mia

Between 1974 and 1982, ABBA were an unstoppable force. They're the third biggest selling singles artist of all time in the UK, with nine number 1s and eight number 1 albums in a row. *Forbes* reports that ABBA made over $2 billion in their career. My, my, that's a lot of spandex money.

'Waterloo' went to number 1 in Belgium, Denmark, Finland, Ireland, the Netherlands, Norway, Switzerland, West Germany and the UK.

Climbing to the top

Laughable Lyrics

Some of the lyrics in Eurovision songs are hilarious because they know it's ridiculous, right?

'Euro-Vision' (1980)
'Eurovision, Eurovision, Eurovision.'
Belgium electro-wonder Telex kept things nice and simple.

'Suus' (2012)
'My plane lands on the runway without the lights of your soul.'
Rona Nishliu's song sounded so cool in Albanian. The translation, um . . .

'Dschinghis Khan' (1979)
'Send for some vodka, ho ho ho ho, cause we're Mongolians ha ha ha ha.'
Historically accurate or not, this disco bop from West Germany's Dschinghis Khan came fourth.

'Flying the Flag (For You)' (2007)
'Would you like something to suck on for landing, sir?'
Yes, Scooch went there.

'Party for Everybody' (2012)
'The cat is happy, the dog is happy, the cat is happy, the dog is happy, we are in a wonderful mood.'
The Russian grannies, aka Buranovskiye Babushki, speak to our very souls.

that We Love

'Technicolour' (2021)
'Time to take off your cloaks.'
Montaigne's time at Hogwarts is over.

'Toy' (2018)
'I'm taking my Pikachu home.'
Guess Netta's gotta catch them all.

'You Are the Only One' (2016)
'Thunder and lightning, it's getting exciting.'
Sergey Lazarev is desperate for a spot of rain in his parched back garden.

'Fuego' (2018)
'You got me pelican fly-fly-flyin''
Thank goodness Elena's ravenous seabird has finally taken flight.

'El Diablo' (2021)
'Hotter than sriracha on our bodies, taco, tamale, yeah, that's my mood.'
She's got hot sauce in her bag, Elena Tsagkrinou.

'Nuku Pommiin' (1982)
'If someone soon throws some nuclear poo here on our Europe, what will you say when we get all the filth on our faces?'
Finland's Kojo came last with this moving poetry.

'Golden Boy' (2015)
'Before I leave, let me show you Tel Aviv.'
Nadav Guedj has the perfect chat-up line. Not too much. An excellent tour guide.

DOUZE FACTS

On a need-to-know-basis – i.e. stuff you NEED to know.

1
Duncan Laurence was unable to pass the Eurovision trophy on to Måneskin in 2021 because he had tested positive for COVID.

2
The ESC was originally a technical experiment in television broadcasting. Yawn!

3
The highest note ever sung at Eurovision is a B6 whistle note sung by Israel's Eden Alene in 2021.

5
The set for the Eurovision final in Moscow in 2009 used 30% of the world's LED screens.

4
The first time Riverdance was performed, was as the 1994 Eurovision interval act.

6
After winning Eurovision in 2004, Ruslana became a deputy member of parliament in Ukraine.

7

Until 1993, the only Eastern bloc country to compete in the competition was Yugoslavia.

9

Cheryl Baker won the contest as part of Bucks Fizz in 1981, but she actually represented the UK in 1978 when she was in the group Co-Co. That band came 11th with their song 'Bad Old Days'.

8

Australia started broadcasting Eurovision in 1983. They had to watch and wait for 32 years before they would be able to enter.

10

Ralph Seigel has written more songs for the contest than any other person: 24, including 1982 winner Nicole's 'Ein bißchen Frieden ('a little peace').

12

When they found themselves in the bottom three in 2021, the heads of the UK and Spanish delegations, Andrew Cartmell and Eva Mora, made a vow to turn their luck around. The following year they were in the top three.

11

British entrant SuRie represented the UK in 2018, but she also provided backing vocals for Belgium's entries in 2015 and 2017.

EURULEVISION

How to win the contest in dix points.

The truth is, there is no rule to winning Eurovision, you just have to hit hard with a song that captures the mood of the night. That said, it pays to be prepared, so here's a 10-point guide to taking the trophy.

Catchy

Be memorable. You've got three minutes to make it stick before Moldova comes on stage dressed as a moose on wheels. Some repetition will be needed, but not so much that you drive the audience insane.

Unique

Nice but generic songs are forgettable. Being a bit weird, like Netta chirping, can work in your favour if the song has a strong melodic underpinning. On the other hand, doing something simple and serious when everyone else is twerking in CGI flames can also work in your favour.

Voice

On the whole, you need a beltingly good set of pipes. Many a potential winning song has been let down by wobbly vocals on the night. Nerves kill dreams.

Emotion

Songs that evoke strong feelings in viewers win. That feeling can be sadness or joy, rebellion or rejection, survival, utter bewilderment or even euphoria. Also, a little signposting never harmed a song.

Anthemic

A winning song will rise and rise to a crescendo that the whole crowd are desperate to sing along to. Eurovision fans want to share a moment, we want to share a chorus – no matter what language it's in.

Charisma

Star power counts, and that comes down to confidence and self-belief. You're a star, act like one. Strut like Damiano David and own the camera.

Spectacle

It's not essential, but this is a show, put one on. Leap and dive, straddle and wiggle. Use all the tools in the staging tool kit. Måns Zelmerlöw's doodle buddy made his performance extra memorable, because it was a total wow moment.

Look

Clothes maketh the song. Sad ballad boys, this doesn't apply to you, but everyone else needs to get a stylist and sort out a wardrobe mood board. This is a massive moment; you need to look your best and not like everyone else, so no beaded dance costumes, no black suits and absolutely no H&M (a tip we took from RuPaul's Drag Race).

English

This rule has been slipping of late, with wins in Italian and Ukrainian, but the fact is most winning songs are still sung in English. When Portugal won in 2017, it was the first time in a decade that a song sung in a language other than English had won. Maybe go the clever route of K-pop bops and sing half in your native tongue and half in English, so everyone can connect with your song's message.

Authentic

Don't sell what you think 'they' want. Follow your vision and passions and be yourself, 100%! Don't hold back. Be Loreen, be a queen.

THEY ARE THE HEROES OF OUR TIME...
SAM RYDER

How did Sam perform for the UK in 2022?
He was up in space, maaaan.

Guitar Hero

Sam was always a fan of Eurovision growing up, but one act made an impact more than most: Lordi. "My favourite Eurovision moment was Lordi's 'Hard Rock Hallelujah'" Sam revealed. He said that he was just starting to learn the guitar, and seeing them in their prosthetics and big platform shoes was inspiring to him.

In 2017, Sam opened a vegan juice bar with his girlfriend.

'Space Man' went to number 2 in the UK chart, making it the highest placed Eurovision song in over 20 years.

Sam (Hair Wolf) Ryder

Sam Ryder is the most followed UK artist on TikTok. Sam was massive on the platform even before he found Eurovision fame, building a huge fanbase during COVID lockdown by singing snippets of songs by the likes of Elton John and Queen, and blowing everyone's socks off.

Hitting all the right notes

Full name: Sam Ryder

ESC song: 'Space Man'

Score: 466 [televote: 183, jury: 283]

Age during ESC: 32

Signature look: Sparkly jumpsuit, long flowing hair, beard, massive great smile

Motto: 'I get "golden retriever energy". And I accept that 100%.'

I'm with the band

Sam has been in more bands than you've had hot showers: Blessed by a Broken Heart, The Morning After, Close Your Eyes and Jupiter Ray, where Sam sang Motown songs for wedding parties. But he found his biggest success in his own bedroom – on TikTok.

Well im-pressed

Sam may not have won Eurovision, but he did win the Marcel Bezençon Press Award for best song. The award, which has been given every year for the last two decades, is given by the media and press attending the event to their favourite song of the contest.

Sam was invited to perform at Queen Elizabeth II's Platinum Jubilee.

'Next year, it's going to be mad. I can't wait to see it … I hope with all my heart that the plethora of talent, the diverse pool of talent that exists in the UK, is going to bust down doors to be part of Eurovision next year.' – Sam Ryder

Jury favourite

The industry juries of 15 countries gave 'Space Man' 12 or 10 points – making his song the 2022 jury favourite of the night. The number of televoting countries to give the song 12 or 10 points, however, was two. This surely indicates that to some extent political voting hindered Sam's chances of winning. The French televote gave Sam 2 points. Zut alors!

10 Artists You

Some stars became so famous that you forgot where they began, while for others their big flash of fame had already passed.

JULIO IGLESIAS
SPAIN, 1970

In 2013, Julio Iglesias was presented with the Guinness World Record for bestselling Latin artist when he sold 250 million albums. Which will take the edge off the fact he only came 4th with his song 'Gwendolyne', looking seriously Gucci. Enrique's dad had it going on.

OLIVIA NEWTON-JOHN
UK, 1974

Four years before Grease, Olivia represented the UK, the year ABBA won. What chance did she have? Her appearance must've played some part in Australia's obsession with the competition. Fact fans might want to note that she performed her song 'Long Live Love' in the dreaded 2nd spot, a position no winner has ever come from.

NANA MOUSKOURI
LUXEMBOURG, 1963

The most famous specs wearer in showbiz, Nana is by some accounts the best-selling female artist of all time, with a reported 350 million albums sold worldwide. With 200 albums recorded in 10 languages, she has to be one of the most successful artists ever to come from the contest. 'I didn't win, I came 8th but I think the exposure was wonderful.'

BACCARA
LUXEMBOURG, 1978

Luxembourg was always pulling out the stops, and in 1978 they managed to bag number one bestselling disco artist Baccara to represent them. Their song, 'Parlez-vous Francais?' coming just months after 'Yes Sir, I Can Boogie' seemed like a surefire win, but the Spanish duo came 7th. Escandalo!

Forgot Entered Eurovision

SAMANTHA JANUS
UK, 1991

In 1991, Ronnie Mitchell from UK TV show *Eastenders* was the bookies' favourite to win the contest: weird, but true. At just eighteen years old, the singing actress had a decent song but ended up in 10th position.

BLACK LACE
UK, 1979

Years before the dreaded 'Agadoo', party band Black Lace were sent to represent the UK in 1979. Perhaps their time at the competition inspired them to make the holiday music they became known for, such as 'Do the Conga' and (eye roll) 'I Speaka da Lingo'. Eesh.

JAVINE
UK, 2005

To pop fans of a certain age, Javine was the girl that was robbed of her place in Girls Aloud; she was the sixth choice. Javine beat Katie Price to represent the UK with her song 'Touch My Fire', but ultimately endured another crushing loss, coming 22nd out of 24. It was the UK's second poorest performance at that point.

T.A.T.U
RUSSIA, 2003

In 2002, t.A.T.u became the first Russian global pop stars, so naturally they were chosen to represent their country the following year. Emo hyper-pop classic 'All the Things She Said' was a number one across the world and their Eurovision entry, 'Ne Ver Ne Boysia', proved it wasn't a one-off fluke. Despite an incredibly pitchy delivery, the duo came third.

LAS KETCHUP
SPAIN, 2006

There was a barely a country in Europe where Las Ketchup's song, 'The Ketchup Song', didn't go to number 1. That was in 2002. Four years later the ketchup had curdled and their song 'Un Bloody Mary' came 21st.

BLUE
UK, 2011

Can you believe the UK's Blue entered Eurovision? It seems like a dream. The boy band who found massive success in the early 2000s were chosen to represent the UK, years after their final hit.

Country Roads:

Ireland has won more times than any country – not

Butch Moore

'Walking the Streets in the Rain', the first song submitted by Ireland, recalled the baroque pop of Burt Bacharach and The Walker Brothers. It did well, coming in 4th.

Dana

'All Kinds of Everything' was Ireland's first ever winning song. The fact that the nineteen-year-old singer was from Northern Ireland caused just a little bit of controversy.

1965

1970

Johnny Logan

'What's Another Year' was Ireland's second winning song. The song was performed 17th – statistically the luckiest place to be.

1980

1994

Paul Harrington and Charlie McGettigan

'Rock 'n' Roll Kids', a nostalgic ballad, gave Ireland a hat trick: three winning songs in a row, something that has never happened again.

1987

1992

1993

Johnny Logan

'Hold Me Now' was Johnny Logan's second winning Eurovision song. He's the only performer to win the competition twice.

Linda Martin

'Why Me', the winning song for 1992, was written by none other than Johnny Logan, who by then knew a thing or two about Eurovision belters.

Niamh Kavanagh

'In Your Eyes', a whacking great power ballad, was the fifth winning song for Ireland. Unbelievably, the dramatic key change was suggested by *Frozen* star Idina Menzel, who sang the original demo.

Eire (Ireland)

that you'd guess from their recent performances.

Eimear Quinn

'The Voice', gave Ireland another win, making the nineties well and truly their decade. With the luck of the Irish and Eurovision placements, how could she fail? Eimear performed 17th.

Lesley Roy

'Story of My Life', Lesley's submission in 2020, had to be scrapped, but she found her way back with 'Maps' in 2021, a wonderful effort – but the staging was OTT and her vocals suffered, meaning Ireland failed to qualify.

1996

2020-2021

Dervish

'They Can't Stop the Spring' was the first time Ireland came last, with a meagre 5 points.

2007

2014 – 2017

Failed to Qualify

After coming last in 2013, Ireland failed to qualify four years in a row, and sadly they've never found their feet again.

2008

Dustin the Turkey

'Irlande Douze Points', was not funny, it was dumb. Maybe Ireland had gotten bored of winning, but with songs like this, they weren't even qualifying.

2011

Jedward

'Lipstick' shouldn't have worked. Twins John and Edward – Jedward – were something of a joke, but Europe enjoyed their Britney-esque song, giving Ireland their best placing in a decade. They came 8th.

THEY ARE THE HEROES OF OUR TIME...
DANA INTERNATIONAL

Eurovision's first out and proud LGBTQ+ winner was proof that the contest was a safe and welcoming place for everyone.

Dana International's Eurovision win has to be one of the most significant in terms of cultural impact. Her win paved the way to understanding and opening the conversation about gender identity.

Fangirl

Sharon grew up watching the Eurovision Song Contest. She remembers Israel's win in 1979, with 'Hallelujah', and Gali Atari from Milk and Honey was especially important to her. 'Eurovision was the biggest evening,' she said. 'We waited the whole year. Everything looked gorgeous. It's a big dream to become a singer at Eurovision.'

Diva Spice

Geri Halliwell left the Spice Girls just days after Dana International won Eurovision and somebody thought Dana would be the perfect replacement. 'I received an invitation to audition to be a member of the Spice Girls, but I don't know if it was really serious,' she told *Attitude* magazine.

Dana the exhibition

Such is her impact that in 2018 an exhibition all about Dana International opened at the Beit Meirov Gallery in Holon near Tel Aviv, which included costumes like her Eurovisionensemble designed by Jean Paul Gaultier.

If you're not wearing a wig and waving a flag, are you even a fan?

Fandemonium

Eurovision fans are the absolute best. They may pick favourites, but they love and support everyone, from first listen until forevermore.

Every fandom will tell you that they're the most passionate, the most obsessed, the most utterly bonkers for their fave. Eurovision fans have got to be right up there with the Whovians, Trekkies, ARMY and Blinks; their devotion, dedication and travel expenses are almost matchless.

Looking for some fashion inspo for your own Eurovision party? What about a flag dress?

A selfie with the winner has got to be the ultimate fan-tasy.

You're a Winner, baby

Snatching trophies is the name of the game.

Eurovision contestants all talk about how it's the participation that counts: making friends, forming a new family and securing a fanbase for life. That's true, but it's also nice to have something shiny to put on the sideboard next to your Funko Pop collection. With stand-out performances, these contestants came to win.

JAMALA
All the emotions, all the pride, probably needs a wee, what a star.

ALEXANDER RYBAK
Look at his little face though. So incredibly happy.

MÅNESKIN
Ethan and Thomas did their best to hold back tears on the night. (ESC rules state that water is not permitted on the stage.)

DUNCAN LAURENCE

Want to know how Duncan has such an amazing voice? He can open his mouth really wide. Science.

NETTA

Netta gave a very moving acceptance speech: 'Quack, quack, ka-ka-kaa.'

LOREEN

The coolest Eurovision winner is cool with it.

CONCHITA WURST

The fist is about to pump a big, YES, another piece of jewellery to add to the box'.

KALUSH ORCHESTRA

A respectfully restrained win for Ukraine.

PRIDE
AT THE HEART OF EUROVISION

Eurovision is sometimes called 'gay Christmas'. But it doesn't stop there. The ESC celebrates everyone under the LGBTQ+ rainbow.

Iceland's Paul Oscar was Eurovision's first 'out' contestant in 1997, closely followed by Katrina of Katrina and the Waves, who won that year. A year later, trans contestant Dana International won, and since then, being part of the LGBTQ+ family has never been an obstacle to showcasing talent. Eurovision sends a yearly message to the world to be your authentic self.

Secret love song

Eurovision's first LGBT anthem 'Nous les amoureux' was sung by the gay actor/singer Jean-Claude Pascal in 1961 and it won. Most people at the time would've been clueless, but watch the clip on YouTube with Google translate and try not to get choked up.

Finland — quite cold, but really cool

Finland is one of the most LGBTQ+ friendly countries in the world. Finnish author and creator of the Moomins, Tove Jansson, is a national hero and she was gay, no big deal. But when Krista Siegfrids performed a cute wedding number in support of marriage equality and kissed another woman in 2013, it caused quite a stir.

ESC's drag place

20 years ago in 2002, Slovenia blazed a trail with a trio of drag queens called Sestre. Their song 'Samo ljubezen' is a forgotten disco gem and possibly inspired Scooch. In 2007, OTT drag performer DQ represented Denmark, with the song, 'Drama Queen'. It probably didn't make it to the Grand Final because Verka Serduchka, another drag queen, was too iconic and split the camp-insanity vote. This of course was all years before RuPaul hit the small screen with her little TV show.

Go off, 2019!!!

2019 was basically a Pride event. Not only did the host talk about his struggle to accept his sexuality, trans pioneer Dana International performed and a kiss-cam zoomed in on gay couples in the audience. The most memorable songs of the night came from artists who sit under the rainbow umbrella: Duncan Laurence (1st), John Lundvik (5th), KEiiNO (6th), Hatari (10th), Bilal (16th), not to mention Mahmood (2nd) who defiantly doesn't define his sexuality.

Come through, 2021

2021 was another good year for the community. 'Amnesia' singer Roxen, from Romania, revealed that they were non-binary. Australia's entrant Sheldon Riley was an openly gay man with Asperger's, and let's not forget Måneskin's Victoria sharing she's bisexual. Ethan is also 'sexually free' and Damiano and Thomas snogged on stage in solidarity.

LED BY EXAMPLE

Like them or not, LED screens have become a big part of Eurovision, the imagery often combining with the song in our minds to add to its lasting impact.

Not every country uses the LED screens in their presentation, but some do and they absolutely become the focus. Some argue that the use of the screens is unfair or even lazy. Without them the performer really has a chance to shine; with them, they face the accusation of being gimmicky. Either way, they add much needed variety and colour to the show.

Stairful how you go

The year after Måns wowed the crowd, Russia's Sergey Lazarev went a step further, incorporating actual stairs into the screens in a death-defying routine that actually saw him fall off them in rehearsals.

On the toon

Måns Zelmerlöw set the standard of what you could do with LED screens in 2015, winning with a little help from his cartoon friends.

House proud

In 2019, Miki bounced around a virtual house – a prediction for the 2020 COVID lockdown?

Flag-shine

Kalush Orchestra made use of 2022's 'the sun within' backdrop set-up to celebrate their national identity, with the colours of Ukraine's flag filling the entire space.

Boxed in

Don't box Gjon's Tears in. OK, do.

Pretty roomy

At first it looks like Rosa Linn is performing in front of a projection of a paper-covered bedroom, until she 'snaps' and starts ripping the walls down to reveal a giant real-life stage set. It proves that sometimes you've gotta keep it real.

- ▶ 2017 saw countries use LED screens with varying creativity

- ▶ In 2018, Lisbon did away with LED screens

- ▶ 2019 saw the biggest LED screen, 36 metres wide and 12 metres high, made up of 16,998,976 pixels, until …

- ▶ The LED screen in Rotterdam in 2021 was 52 metres wide and 12 metres high

U OK HUN?

Just some Eurovision kings and queens doing the absolute most.

Why sing a nice song in a single spotlight when you can ride a unicycle in a dunce's cap? Maybe some ideas are lost in translation, or maybe we just don't know genius when we see it. Welcome to the most chaotic Eurovision moments ever.

RYKKA, SWITZERLAND, 2016

Setting fire to your entrant's head is audacious. You can't argue with that.

JEDWARD, IRELAND, 2012

Water is banned at Eurovision after John and Edward's fountain flooded the stage.

TRIANA PARK, LATVIA, 2017

Bit of Gaga, smidge of Katy Perry and just a pinch of Bride of Chucky.

SVETLANA LOBODA, UKRAINE, 2009

Svetlana, you in danger, gurl! (I don't think these are real Roman centurions.)

O.TORVALD, UKRAINE, 2017

Gonna tell my kids this is how we told the time before Apple watches.

ZLATA OGNEVICH, UKRAINE, 2013

Zlata loved being carried in by the world's hugest man. Look at her face. Not panicking at all.

ZDOB ȘI ZDUB, MOLDOVA, 2011

As distraction techniques go, this rigmarole is pretty entertaining.

DANIEL DIGES, SPAIN, 2010

Forget honey and ginger, a deranged court jester panting in your face will make you sing better.

STEFANIA, GREECE, 2021

Behind every great woman there's a man in a lime green lycra bodysuit.

Totally Instrumental

C'mon, everyone, let's make some noise.

Until 1998, Eurovision provided a full orchestra. Today the music is all on backing tracks. Instruments aren't exactly mimed, but you won't ever hear the live sound an on-stage instrument makes. Perhaps that's why so many crop up, because if you can't actually play the ukulele, who's going to know?

Iceland has never won Eurovision – perhaps if they made a bit less racket.

Alexander Rybak made violins cool. Not cool-cool or street cool, but Eurovision cool, which is definitely not an oxymoron.

Oh Lordi! Wait till he realises his axe isn't plugged in.

Ovi's circular piano is iconic. Unplayable and extremely cumbersome, but just look at it.

Somebody's seen Kate Bush's 'Babooshka' video. That somebody is Ana Rucner.

Freddie famously lifted his shirt up in every performance. Apparently, there was a giant gong drum as well.

Calm down, Elena, it's just bagpipes, an accordion and whatever that other thing is.

Movie Night

NOBODY WINS SOLO

WILL FERRELL   RACHEL McADAMS

EUROVISION
SONG CONTEST
THE STORY OF FIRE SAGA

JUNE 26 | NETFLIX

Is the Eurovision film worth watching? Ja ja ding dong!

Eurovision fans were anxious when Netflix released *The Eurovision Song Contest: The Story of Fire Saga*, but they needn't have worried. It was a silly but ultimately loving homage to the greatest show on earth with some actually decent songs. The story follows Icelandic Eurovision superfans Lars (Will Ferrell) and Sigrit (Rachel McAdams), who've always dreamed of performing at the ESC with their band Fire Saga. Through a series of calamitous events, it actually happens. The movie is a lot of fun, not least because it's packed with in-jokes, such as Will Ferrell rolling off stage in a hamster wheel, like Ukraine's 2014 entry. Oh – and there's a ton of familiar faces.

Rachel McAdams' singing is provided by Swedish singer and ESC hopeful Molly Sanden.

Will Ferrell became a fan of Eurovision after being introduced to the competition by his Swedish wife, Viveca Paulin. He saw the 2014 Grand Final in Copenhagen and went again in 2018 to Lisbon, even being given permission to watch the rehearsals.

Netta Barzilai delivers a unique twist on Black Eyed Peas.

Some scenes were filmed during Eurovision 2019.

For the rousing 'song-along' party scene, former contestants sing a mash-up of tunes including ABBA's 'Waterloo' and Celine Dion's 'Ne partez pas sans moi'.

Winners' circle: Conchita, Rachel McAdams and Loreen.

Downton Abbey's Dan Stevens plays rival Russian singer Alexander Lemtov who is clearly taking inspiration from the shirt-defying talents of Dima Bilan and two-times ESC performer Sergey Lazarev.

Cameos in the film

► Alexander Rybak, Norway
► Conchita Wurst, Austria
► Jamala, Ukraine
► Loreen, Sweden
► Netta, Israel
► Salvador Sobral, Portugal

Fan faves

► Anna Odobescu, Moldova
► Bilal, France
► Elina Nechayeva, Serbia
► Jessy Matador, France
► John Lundvik, Sweden
► Demi Lovato

FUEGO

They're burning up and they ain't cooling down.

The Makemakes scored nil-points in 2015, but they will go down in ESC history for setting fire to a piano, and that's what counts.

The camera doesn't lie. When Alexander Rybak plays, sparks fly.

You expect flames at a rock performance, and who are Måneskin to let you down?

KEiiNO had one of the most dramatic songs of the night in 2019, so of course they had massive plumes of fire. Norway's never been so hot.

In 2018, Melovin took the fiery piano motif and, well, added more fire. Scorchio.

Senhit got the audience's adrenalina pumping with fire and gasolina, quite literally.

Jaguar Jones came third in Eurovision: Australia Decides in 2022 with her song 'Little Fires', and even though she didn't officially make the ESC, her flaming dress won't be forgotten in a hurry.

When Efendi sangs 'I start a fire' in her song 'Mata Hari', fire filled the stage. Sometimes a literal interpretation is the way to go.

FUN WITH FLAGS

Recognise the flags of participating Eurovision nations at a glance with this handy guide.

Switzerland is the only country in Eurovision to have a square flag.

Israel is the only flag to represent an associated religion of the country: the six-pointed star of David and Judaism.

The Union Jack was introduced in 1801 and references England, Scotland and Ireland. Sorry, Wales.

Emblems on flags are called 'charges'. Cut-outs (like the stars on Australia's flag) are called 'cantons'. Vertical stripes are referred to as 'pales' and a horizontal stripe is called a 'fess'.

The study of flags is called vexillology.

Denmark has the oldest flag in the world, first appearing in 1219.

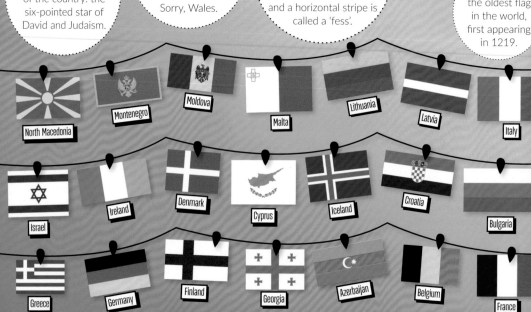

Full name: Sharon Cohen

ESC song: 'Diva'

Score: 172

Age during ESC: 29

Signature look: A bird of paradise about to take flight (a feathered dress)

Motto: 'My victory proves God is on my side.'

Dana's biggest inspiration is Israeli singer Ofra Haza.

Ding dong! Dana International makes her 2011 comeback

After Netta's win in 2018, the contest returned to Israel and of course Dana International performed.

Before Eurovision, Dana was a well-known singer in Israel.

Return to Eurovision

Many contestants miss the thrill of Eurovision and can't help but go back. For Dana it proved to be something of a disappointment. Her return in 2011 was welcomed, but the song 'Ding Dong' failed to move beyond the semi-finals.

Belle of the nineties

Armchair critics love to write off Dana International's Eurovision win, claiming that 'her story' was the reason she won. This misses the point entirely. Dana International's song 'Diva' was remarkable because it was a banging anthem that connected with a younger audience. A combination many competitors have tried, and failed, to achieve.

'People don't care about my voice. They care that I speak my opinion, without fear. They'll say I'm so brave, blah blah blah. I'm just living my life, and it's not an easy life.' – Dana International

COUNTRY ROADS: NORGE (NORWAY)

Unlike their neighbour Sweden, Norway has had one of the roughest Eurovision journeys.

1960–1961
Joining in

Norway joined the Eurovision family in its fifth year with a song called 'Voi Voi' sung by Nora Brockstedt. Nora came 4th out of 13, not bad for a first try, so she was sent back to represent Norway again in 1961, but came 7th.

1963
Oh nil!

Norway received their first ever score of nil-points with 'Solhverv', sung by Anita Thallaug. Unlike Nora Brockstedt, she was not invited back the following year.

1966
Åse Kleveland

For decades, 'Intet er nytt under solen' by Å se Kleveland was Norway's most successful entry, coming 3rd. Expressive, dramatic, cinematic, the song sounded like it was lifted from a Western. Åse was the first female singer to play the guitar and the first to wear trousers. Trailblazer!

1985 Bobbysocks!

Norway's first win! And what fun! 'La Det Swinge' ('Let it Swing') by female duo Bobbysocks! was a rock 'n roll throwback that could've come from the *Grease* soundtrack, if Danny and Sandy had gone to school in Oslo.

1995
Secret Garden

Despite a history of doing terribly, Norway still takes chances and that's incredibly inspiring. When they entered with 'Nocturne' by Secret Garden, the chillest song ever, with the fewest words ever, it could have totally bombed, but the gamble paid off and it won.

2009
Alexander Rybak

When Alexander Rybak's 'Fairytale' gave Norway its third Eurovision win, it did so with a bang, gaining 387 points – the most ever received up to that point. Alexander Rybak's average score from each voting nation was 9.4 and he received sixteen sets of douze points, another record. The song was so popular it even made the UK top 10.

2019
KEiiNO

2019 could've been Norway's year. 'Spirit in the Sky' by KEiiNO is easily one of the best Eurovision anthems of recent years and a clear example of how the jury can get it SO wrong. KEiiNO won the 2019 public televote with 291 points. Yet they received a measly 40 points from the juries. Wrong!

Norway's Anne-Karine is the only Eurovision act to come last twice – in 1974 and 1976.

2022
Subwoolfer

Once again proving that Norway marches to the beat of its own drum, the Norwegian delegation sent the song 'Give That Wolf a Banana', sung by a band dressed as bright yellow wolves with the funniest lyrics ever: 'Not sure you have a name, so I will call you Keith.' Keep being weird, Norway, we love it.

Norway has come last in the Eurovision Grand Final a record-breaking 11 times. Not a record they probably want.

THEY ARE THE HEROES OF OUR TIME...

MAHMOOD

Mahmood has done that very rare thing: delivered two incredible Eurovision songs. Could we ever hope for a third?

X marks the spot

Did you know that Mahmood first found fame in Italy 10 years ago on the Italian version of *The X Factor*? He made it to judges' houses and then to live shows as a wild card, but was quickly eliminated.

Mahmood is the sign of the times Harry Styles once sang about. Like Måneskin, his music is not typical Italian pop music, but an anything-goes fusion of pop, hip hop and electro, incorporating influences from his Arabic and Italian heritage. When he arrived at Eurovision in 2019, not everyone got it, but he was so chill and effortlessly cool it served as a palate cleanser, the likes of which hadn't been seen since Loreen.

Mahmood was named as one of the *Forbes* 30 Under 30, making him one of the most influential young people in Italy.

Italy: not entirely sold on 'Soldi'

The Italian public don't know what they want. At the Festival di Sanremo, the Italian national selection show, 'Soldi' was a hit with the professional juries, but the televoting public put Mahmood in 7th place. Crazy! Fast forward a couple of months and, oh look, 'Soldi' is number one in Italy.

'People are just people. It's not important where you come from, where you are – it's important where you're going.' – Mahmood

Full name: Alessandro Mahmood

ESC song: 'Soldi' ('Money')

Score: 472 points

Age during ESC: 26

Signature look: A jazzy shirt and a buzzcut with a straight fringe

Motto: 'If you don't take a risk, you are already dead.'

2015 winner Måns Zelmerlöw named 'Soldi' as one of his favourite Eurovision songs of all time. 'This song is so good,' he said in 2021.

'Soldi' received 10 sets of douze points at the Eurovision final. Neither the UK jury nor the UK televoting public gave the song any points. Scandalo!

His follow-up song, 'Brividi', broke Italian Spotify records for the most streams in a day.

Things got real

Even if you speak Italian, it's not instantly obvious why 'Soldi' was so impactful and unusual a Eurovision entry. The song tells the complicated autobiographical story of a father who has left his son and wife to live a new life and has basically stopped caring about them. It's painful and specific. Even without a translation we can hear every single emotion in Mahmood's heartfelt delivery.

Instaban?

When Mahmood and Blanco posed naked on the cover of Italian *Vanity Fair*, Instagram allegedly removed the image from Mahmood's stories, saying it 'violated guidelines'. *Vanity Fair* reposted the image with the word 'censored' over the duo and went on a mini-rant. The adage 'all publicity is good publicity' was proven to be true when the image became a viral sensation.

Mahmood has had three number 1s in Italy – 'Soldi', 'Brividi' and 'Calipso'.

Style icon

Mahmood is a proper pop star. He doesn't only make record-breaking music, he looks flawlessly fabulous doing it. You can spot him on the front row of fashion shows like Prada, Fendi and Balmain, see him wearing designer gear like Margiela and MGSM and even catch him walking the runway for Burberry, who chose him to model for them twice.

The iconic double-hand clap in action

FIVE HOT TAKES FROM EUROVISION COMMENTATORS

In 2022, BBC reporter Mark Savage got ESC TV commentators to reveal what it's like working on the big night. Here are our hot takeaways.

'We're right at the top under the roof. Every country has little tiny, tiny cabins together…'
– Stephane Bern (France) on working conditions

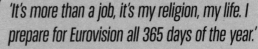

'It's more than a job, it's my religion, my life. I prepare for Eurovision all 365 days of the year.'
– Timur Miroshnychenko (Ukraine) on doing what he (and we) love

Graham Norton, the star of the show for many UK viewers

THREE GRAHAM NORTON QUIPS

1. 'If you're watching with pets or sensitive older people, maybe now's the time to put them in the utility room.'
on Cezar's 'It's My Life' from Romania

2. 'The bad news is, you're about to watch Albania.'
on Kejsi Tola in 2009

3. 'If it doesn't work out for him, he's always got his hotel management degree. I feel he's going to use it.'
on Hungary's 2016 contestant, Freddie

> 'I try and visit every single rehearsal. The more info I have, the more relaxed I'll feel when it's time to go live.'
> — Edward af Sillén (Sweden) on knowing the show inside out

> 'We help each other with jokes, news and information; there is always an extremely friendly atmosphere.'
> — Peter Urban (Germany) on commentator camaraderie

Terry Wogan, the face of Eurovision

TERRY WOGAN'S VISION OF EUROVISION

El Tel was the UK's commentator from 1971 to 2008, and boy did he speak his mind.

'Who knows what hellish future lies ahead?
Actually, I do, I've seen the rehearsals.'
in 2007

'Every year I expect it to be less foolish and
every year it is more so.'
on Finnish winners, Lordi, in 2006

'No, it's not Rita from *Coronation Street*.'
on Russia's 1997 entry, Alla Pugacheva

'I love the Eurovision Song Contest and it will
continue long after I'm gone.'
on why he did it for so long

The only living person to host the contest more than once is Petra Mede of Sweden. She hosted the contest alone in 2013 and with winner Måns Zelmerlöw in 2016.

STORY OF A WINNING SONG:
'MAKING YOUR MIND UP'
BY BUCKS FIZZ

The boy-girl-boy-girl formula delivers another iconic winner for the UK.

If you said 'Eurovision' to passing strangers on the average British high street, a lot of people would say 'Bucks Fizz' back to you. Bucks Fizz are the quintessential Eurovision act because they were formed specifically for the contest, won, and built an entire career based on it.

★ Close call

For such an iconic winner, 'Making Your Mind Up' had a real battle to the finish line. Bucks Fizz finished with 136 points, but just behind them were Germany with 132, France with 125 and Switzerland with 121.

Bucks Fizz had three UK number 1 singles, 'Making Your Mind Up', 'Land of Make Believe' and 'My Camera Never Lies'.

Legs out for the win

Skirting the issue

According to Cheryl Baker, the infamous skirt-ripping dance routine came about by total accident. Discussing what to wear, Jay Aston said she wanted to wear a short skirt while Cheryl said she wanted to wear a long one. When Cheryl shrugged and said, 'Let's have both,' she meant one of each, but their choreographer was like, 'That's it!'

Total points: 136
Number of douze points awarded: 2
Performance position: 14th
UK chart: 1st
Band line-up: Jay Aston, Cheryl Baker, Bobby G, Mike Nolan

'We won Eurovision by 4 points: that's down to Velcro.' – Cheryl Baker

Tuned out

Cheryl Baker famously says that she sang the whole song at Eurovision in a different key to the rest of the band because of nerves and Mike Nolan says it was something they teased her for, for years. 'I still rib Cheryl about her singing out of tune,' he joked back in 2016.

Dreams do come true

Back in the day, Eurovision was hugely aspirational. 'When I was about nine I had a little book and I had a list of all the things I wanted to achieve,' Jay Aston said in 2021. 'I had "win the Eurovision Song Contest", "be on *Top of the Pops* with a number one record" and "do the Royal Command".' She achieved all of those things by the time she was 21.

The song fizzes along

'Making Your Mind Up' seems like a pretty innocuous pop song about someone who blows hot and cold in a relationship, but right from the opening glam-rock drumroll, it's actually quite clever, doing exactly what the lyrics suggest, speeding things up and then slowing things down. The words "making your mind up" serve as a false ending because the song loops around and keeps going.

'Making Your Mind Up' was the natural choice of names for the UK's TV selection programme and was used from 2004 to 2007.

SELECT-A-SONG CONTEST

Eurovision isn't just a week, it's at least half a year!

Many countries host their own show to choose the artist and song that will be sent to represent them at Eurovision. Some of the shows are massively popular and, let's be honest, enviable events. The two most famous preliminary music competitions are Melodifestivalen in Sweden and the Festival di Sanremo in Italy. It's no wonder these countries consistently do well; they take it very seriously.

Cornelia Jakobs beat thousands to win Melodifestivalen 2022

Melodifestivalen

The 'melody festival' has been going on since 1959 and is one of the most popular TV shows in Sweden. Like Eurovision itself, the results are determined by a panel of judges and viewer votes. The show airs on TV over six weeks and approximately a third of the songs must be in Swedish, which is strange because almost no Swedish songs ever make it to Eurovision. The winner receives the 'Great Songbird' trophy.

20 selection shows to stream online

Estonia: Eesti Laul
Croatia: Dora Music Festival
Denmark: Dansk Melodi Grand Prix
Finland: Uuden Musiikin Kilpailu (UMK)
France: C'est vous qui décidez
Germany: Germany 12 Points
Iceland: Söngvakeppnin
Ireland: The Late, Late Show Eurosong Special
Czech Republic: ESCZ
Italy: Festival di Sanremo
Latvia: Supernova
Lithuania: Pabandom iš naujo
Moldova: O Melodie pentru Europa
Norway: Melodi Grand Prix
Portugal: Festival da Canção
Romania: Selecția Națională
Slovenia: EMA Freš
Spain: Benidorm Fest
Sweden: Melodifestivalen
Ukraine: Vidbir

Festival di Sanremo

The Sanremo Music Festival is the longest-running TV music competition in the world, and one of the longest-running TV shows, full stop. It started in 1951 as an excuse to boost morale and tourism post WWII, and was basically the inspiration for Eurovision. Some international artists who've sung at the festival include Britney Spears, Kylie Minogue, Katy Perry, Shakira and Jennifer Lopez. Beat that, Glastonbury!

PREDICTIONS FOR EUROVISION 2023

Come back when it's all over and see how many came true.

1. At least six songs will be major chart hits across Europe.

2. Bad news for sad ballads: more uplifting bops will make the Grand Final than in 2022.

3. There will be fewer novelty acts this year, with every country in it to win it.

4. Israel will have a massive year with Noa Kirel and will be in the top five.

5. Spain's entry will ramp up the energy with a song that makes J-Lo jealous.

6. Germany will scrape into the left-hand side of the scoreboard.

7. Aussie hopeful Andrew Lambrou will put on a good show for Cyprus, but will not bring home their first win.

8. The UK will have a decent song and place in the top 10, but won't be as successful as Sam Ryder.

9. Ukraine will be in the top 10 again and they will deserve it.

10. Some combo of Jamala, Kalush Orchestra, Ruslana, Go_A and Verka Serduchka will perform at the show's opening.

11. Since the contest takes place in Liverpool, The Beatles will be referenced – more than once, and 1993 UK entry Sonia will be present.

12. Mia and Dion, the duo put together by Duncan Laurence for the Netherlands entry, will be fantastic – but not everyone can win.

13. The interval act will be a huge UK star – Harry Styles, Dua Lipa . . . Paul McCartney?

14. Despite being in England, there will be fewer songs sung in English than usual.

15. A UK host such as Rylan or Claudia Winkleman will host alongside Ukrainian presenter Timur Miroshnychenko.

16. Sweden will not make the top 5 for a change.

THEY ARE THE HEROES OF OUR TIME....
NETTA

Netta is Eurovision's unrivalled baka-bakum, bak-bakumbai, and I think we can all agree on that.

Burger off!

If you ever think someone is trying to pinch your chips at Maccy D's, maybe it's just Netta eavesdropping on your convo. In an Ask Me Anything Reddit Q&A in 2019, she said she is inspired by: 'The people I see at McDonald's.'

A total White off

It would be hard to imagine a world where The White Stripes would win Eurovision, but after spotting a similarity between 'Toy' and 'Seven Nation Army' by indie rock group The White Stripes, Jack White was given a co-writing credit.

Loopy tunes

Netta is a looping artist, which means she records multiple sounds live on a loop station, layering them up into a cohesive rhythm that she then performs with as backing track.

'Thank you so much for choosing difference.' – Netta

Netta officially has the X Factor

In 2021, Netta was set to become an *X Factor* judge alongside Simon Cowell. Simon pulled out at the last minute, but Netta went on to be a memorable judge.

The taste of success is sweet for Netta

Full name: Netta Barzilai

ESC song: 'Toy'

Score: 529 [televote: 317, jury: 212]

Age during ESC: 25

Signature look: Kimono and double space buns in her hair.

Motto: 'You don't have to fit the normal, standard model of how a person should look, think, talk and create in order to succeed.'

No clucking way

Netta's winning Eurovision song about female empowerment, 'Toy', was instantly iconic in no small part due to the singer making bird-like vocalisations. Netta added her infamous chicken-like clucking to the song to tease people who allow themselves to be treated like a toy.

Hometown hero

In her homeland of Israel, Netta was far from a one-hit wonder. Of course, 'Toy' went to number 1, but her follow-up singles 'Bassa Sababa', 'Ricki Lake' and 'Cuckoo' all went to number 1 on Israel's pop chart too.

COUNTRY ROADS: ITALIE (ITALY)

Italy entered every Eurovision Song Contest until 1980 – then it was an on and off affair.

Gigliola Cinquetti returned in 1974, 10 years after her historic win

1951

Five years before Eurovision launched, Italy began a song contest called the Festival di Sanremo, which was the inspiration for Eurovision.

1956

Italy was there at the very first contest. Records of points awarded have been lost, so no one knows how well any country fared, apart from the winning country, Switzerland.

1958
Domenico Modugno

'Volare' aka 'Nel blu, dipinto di blu' only came 3rd, but it's arguably the most well-known Eurovision song next to Waterloo by ABBA. The song was the biggest-selling record in America in 1958, and won both song of the year and record of the year at the first ever Grammy Awards in 1959. It remains the only Eurovision song to have received a Grammy.

1964
Gigliola Cinquetti

When the delicate ballad 'Non Ho L'età', ('I'm Not Old Enough to Love You') by 16'year-old Gigliola won Euro-vision she was the youngest ever winner. She definitely started the trend for teenage girls winning the contest with France Gall following in 1965, Sandie Shaw in 1967 and Dana in 1970.

1966
Last in show

By a weird twist of fate, the only time Italy scored nil-points and came last was with a song sung by one of the biggest stars of Eurovision, Domenico Modugno. 'Dio, come ti amo's' final placing must've come as a blow for the 'Volare' hero.

1974
Second time/second place

The second time Gigliola Cinquetti entered the contest, she came second – to ABBA – so not a bad showing then. Her song 'Si', got to number 8 in the UK chart.

1981–1982

Italy pulled out of the contest without explanation for the first time.

1990
Toto Cutugno

It's strange with hindsight to think that Italy's winning entry, 'Insieme: 1992', a song about bringing Europe together, came from the country famous for flouncing off and refusing to participate in the single greatest event that brings Europe together.

1997
Arrivederci

Italy, a country that had consistently done quite well at Eurovision, said goodbye to the contest for over a decade and a half. With their own super successful Sanremo Music Festival, perhaps they felt they didn't need it.

2011
Buonasera

After a 14-year absence, Italy returned to Eurovision as one of the Big Five with 'Follia d'amore' ('Madness of Love'), a big band, piano-led swing-a-long by Raphael Gualazzi, and everyone was so glad to have them back that the song came 2nd.

2019
Mahmood

'Soldi' ('Money') was the bookies' favourite to win. The intimate, slow-building ballad was a huge record, but on the night, Mahmood didn't quite deliver the perfect vocal and that might've counted against him.

2021
Måneskin

Not only did Måneskin's win show that Italy's investment in the contest had paid off, but they helped make the contest look cool. If a charismatic and current rock band can enter the contest and win, then no act need moan about their credibility being damaged by entering.

2022
Mahmood and Blanco

Mahmood returned to Eurovision after failing to win, and failed to win again, except he didn't really because 'Brividi' ('Chills'), the song he sang with nineteen-year-old Blanco, was a tear-jerking belter that broke the Italian Spotify record for most streams in a day.

TOP 50 EUROVISI

1. 'Soldi', Mahmood, Italy, 2019
2. 'Waterloo', ABBA, Sweden, 1974
3. 'Euphoria', Loreen, Sweden, 2012
4. 'Fairytale', Alexander Rybak, Norway, 2009
5. 'Think About Things', Daði Freyr, Iceland, 2020
6. 'Arcade', Duncan Laurence, Netherlands, 2019
7. 'Fuego', Eleni Foureira, Portugal, 2018
8. 'SHUM', Go_A, Ukraine, 2021
9. 'Poupée de cire, poupée de son', France Gall, Luxembourg, 1965
10. 'Occidentali's Karma', Italy, 2017
11. 'Zitti e Buoni', Måneskin, Italy, 2021
12. 'Space Man', Sam Ryder, UK, 2022
13. 'Spirit in the Sky', KEiiNO, Norway, 2019
14. 'J'ai cherché', Amir, France, 2016
15. 'Heroes', Måns Zelmerlöw, Sweden, 2015
16. 'Voilà', Barbara Pravi, France, 2021
17. 'I Can't Go On', Robin Bengtsson, Sweden, 2017
18. 'The Sound of Silence', Dami Im, Australia, 2016
19. 'I Feel Alive', Imri, Israel, 2017
20. 'Making Your Mind Up', Bucks Fizz, UK, 1981
21. 'Ooh Aah . . . Just a Little Bit', Gina G, UK, 1996
22. 'Save Your Kisses for Me', Brotherhood of Man, UK, 1976
23. 'Ne partez pas sans moi', Celine Dion, Switzerland, 1988
24. 'She Got Me', Luca Hänni, Switzerland, 2019
25. 'One Step Closer', Bardo, UK, 1982
26. '1944', Jamala, Ukraine, 2016
27. 'Brividi', Mahmood and Blanco, Italy, 2022
28. 'Diva', Dana International, Israel, 1998
29. 'J'aime l vie', Sandra Kim, Belgium, 1986
30. 'Toy', Netta, Israel, 2018

31. 'Zero Gravity', Kate Miller-Heidke, Australia, 2019
32. 'What About My Dreams', Kati Wolf, Hungary, 2011
33. 'Replay', Tamta, Cyprus, 2019
34. 'El Diablo', Elena Tsagkrinou, Cyprus, 2021
35. 'Hi', Ofra Haza, Israel, 1983
36. 'Dancing Lasha Tumbai', Verka Serduchka, Ukraine, 2007
37. 'Only Teardrops', Emmelie de Forest, 2013
38. 'Rock Bottom', Lynsey de Paul and Mike Moran, UK, 1977
39. 'Je me casse', Destiny, Malta, 2021
40. 'Rhythm Inside', Loïc Nottet, Belgium, 2015
41. 'Rise Like a Phoenix', Conchita Wurst, Austria, 2014
42. 'I'm Never Giving Up', Sweet Dreams, UK, 1983
43. 'If Love Was a Crime', Poli Genova, Bulgaria, 2016
44. 'Volare' (aka 'Nel blu, dipinto di blu') Domenico Modugno, Italy, 1958
45. 'Truth', Chingiz, Azerbaijan, 2019
46. 'Lipstick', Jedward, Ireland, 2011
47. 'Moustache', Twin Twin, France, 2014
48. 'Øve Os På Hinanden', Fyr Og Flamme, Denmark, 2021
49. 'Ding-a-Dong', Teach-In, Netherlands, 1975
50. 'Hard Rock Hallelujah', Lordi, Finland, 2006

MY EUROVISION TOP 20
Grab a piece of paper and write down your top 20 songs.

1.	6.	11.	16
2.	7.	12.	17.
3.	8.	13.	18
4.	9.	14.	19.
5.	10.	15.	20.

113

TEST YOUR EUROVISION KNOWLEDGE

20 QUESTIONS

Are you a true Eurovision fan?

1 Which Eurovision smash ends with the final words ' …and I want to go home'?

2 Which two years did Johnny Logan win?

3 Why are the numbers 9 and 11 special?

4 How many winning Eurovision songs have there been (up to and including 2022)?
A: 66 B: 68 C: 69

5 How many Eurovisions have there been (up to and including 2022)?
A: 66 B: 68 C: 69

6 What does Måneskin mean in English?
A: Dandruff B: Moonlight C: MySpace

7 What does 'Soldi' mean in English?
A: Burning B: Gentle C: Money

8 Finish the lyric: 'I see your spirit in the sky…'

9

Which country won with a song from a girl called France?

10

Which act, named after a poorly spelled star sign, gave the UK its first 'nil-points'?

11

In 2022, Kalush Orchestra sold their Eurovision trophy to help the war in Ukraine. How much did they get for it?
A: $9,000 B: $90,000
C: $900,000

12

Which country was not in the first Eurovision?
A: Germany B: Norway
C: Switzerland

13

Which city did ABBA win in?
A: Bristol B: Birmingham
C: Brighton

14

Which Irish and Israeli winners share the same first name?

15

Which Eurovision winner recorded their version of Euphoria in 2017?
A: Nicole B: Lulu
C: Celine Dion

16

In 1990 Eurovision introduced a mascot. What was it called?
A: Eurocar B: Eurocat
C: Eurobug

17

What links Greece's 2021 entry and Ukraine's 2022 entry?

18

Which Eurovision song was the most played on UK radio and TV in 2021?
A: Ooh Aah … Just a Little Bit
B: Waterloo C: Think About Things

19

Destiny and Cornelia Jakobs were born 10 years apart, but who was born in 1992 and who was born in 2002?

20

How does Surie write her name?
A: SuriE B: SuRie
C: SUrie

How many did you get right? Answers on page 158

How to Host Your Own Watch Party

You can't watch Eurovision alone. You have to throw a party.
Try these top tips for one epic night!

INVITATIONS

Invite all your Eurovision pals. Especially the ones that will really get into it and help you learn Moldova's complex choreography.

DECORATIONS

Flagging this here and now: you need flags. Flags to hang as bunting and maybe even some stand-alones for people to wave. They're literally the only decorations that are key for Eurovision party success. If you want to go all out, then give your party the host country as a theme. It's a UK and Ukraine mash-up in 2023, so why not hang Ukrainian flags and pictures of The Beatles?

AFTERPARTY

Have a YouTube playlist ready to go with all your favourite Eurovision classics. The show ends at midnight, but that doesn't mean you can't keep dancing until late into the night (12.15 for me!).

DRINK

Eurovision is the perfect opportunity to make up your own non-alcoholic cocktails. Why not try the Ukraineade, lemonade with beetroot? Borscht-licious.

FOOD

Ask everyone to bring a dish from a country of their choice or order in from a couple of local takeaways – everyone has a delivery app on their phone, right?

SCORECARDS

Photocopy the scorecard at the back of this book for everyone to fill in while they watch the show. You can compare scores at the end and see who came closest to predicting the top 5. This is a great activity for during the lengthy jury voting portion. (Don't forget pencils/pens.)

DRESS CODE

Each guest can pick a country or act to dress up as. It might be worth disclosing who you're coming as before the night: Hello 'Night of a Thousand Conchitas'.

THREE HOUSE RULES

You will definitely need to set some ground rules.

1. Talking
Inevitably some people will be more into chatting than watching. These people need to go to the kitchen and everyone must wait till they've heard one verse and one chorus before they slag a song off.

2. Singing along
People will have their faves. They will want to join in, so pop the subtitles on if you want to actually know the words.

3. Dancing
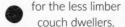
You must allow your guests to dance to the bops, just kindly suggest they don't block the TV for the less limber couch dwellers.

SWEEPSTAKE

Up the stakes and have your own contest. Write down the names of all competing countries and put them in a bowl. Get every attendee to bring a small gift (snacks always preferable!) to put into a bucket. Whoever picks the winning country wins the bucket of prizes.

EUROVISION BINGO

It's the night of the Grand Final. Time to play a game within the game.

Sad-boy ballad	An accordion	Baltic rap
Foreign language song with a chorus in English	Barefoot singer	Tears
A violin	Smoke machine/ dry ice	Dressed in all white
Dancers lift female singer	Dancers paw male singer	Emo rock
Opera aria	Unidentified brass instrument	Wind machine

It's not that Eurovision is predictable, it's that there is only so much you can do to make 40+ songs and performances different to each other year in, year out, and frankly, some staging choices just work. It's not a cliché, it's a tradition.

Photocopy this scorecard and grab a pen. Every time you see something on screen that corresponds to something on the bingo card, cross it out. If you hit 20, then the year is a certified classic!

Someone on wheels	Pointing directly to camera	Fire
Interacting with the VR screen	Gender-defying fashion	Dance-pop lady banger
Bagpipes	Key change	Middle-eastern ethno-pop anthem
National costumes are worn	A woman whips her huge hair	A man whips his huge hair
Gratuitous bum wiggle	Animal costume	Terrifying contestant to give children nightmares

Grand FINAL SCORESHEET

	Song	Vocals	Staging	Points	Final Ranking
01 Country Artist Title					
02 Country Artist Title					
03 Country Artist Title					
04 Country Artist Title					
05 Country Artist Title					
06 Country Artist Title					

If you're reading this in early 2023, the first semi is on 9 May.

How to fill in your score sheet

First, fill in the name of the country, song and artist. Next, score the performance from 1 to 12 points, on how good the song is, how well the artist sang and how exciting their performance was to watch. Then add up the points for a subtotal. Do this for every entry. After all the performances have finished, work out your own personal rankings of who came 1st, 2nd and 3rd, etc, and compare them to how the artists actually score in the show.

Photocopy the next three pages and fill in as you watch along.

	Song	Vocals	Staging	Points	Final Ranking
07 Country Artist Title					
08 Country Artist Title					
09 Country Artist Title					

Notes
Scribble any thoughts you have on the Grand Final here.

Grand FINAL SCORESHEET

		Song	Vocals	Staging	Points	Final Ranking
10	Country Artist Title					
11	Country Artist Title					
12	Country Artist Title					
13	Country Artist Title					
14	Country Artist Title					
15	Country Artist Title					

Cross out the 11 countries below that didn't qualify

Albania • Armenia • Australia • Austria • Azerbaijan • Belgium • Croatia •
Cyprus Czech Republic • Denmark • Estonia • Finland • Georgia • Germany •
Greece Iceland • Ireland • Israel • Italy • Latvia • Lithuania • Malta • Moldova
• Netherlands • Norway • Poland • Portugal • Romania • San Marino • Serbia
Slovenia • Spain • Sweden • Switzerland • Ukraine • United Kingdom

		Song	Vocals	Staging	Points	Final Ranking
16	Country Artist Title					
17	Country Artist Title					
18	Country Artist Title					

Notes

Scribble any thoughts you have on the Grand Final here.

Grand FINAL SCORESHEET

	Song	Vocals	Staging	Points	Final Ranking
19 Country Artist Title					
20 Country Artist Title					
21 Country Artist Title					
22 Country Artist Title					
23 Country Artist Title					
24 Country Artist Title					

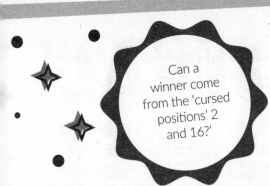

Can a winner come from the 'cursed positions' 2 and 16?

How will the Big Five do this year? Can Germany finally get a decent placing? It's too exciting to bear.

		Song	Vocals	Staging	Points	Final Ranking
25	Country					
	Artist					
	Title					
26	Country					
	Artist					
	Title					

Notes

Scribble any thoughts you have on the Grand Final here.

EUROVISION QUIZ CONTEST
Answers

1. 'Space Man', Sam Ryder
2. 1980, 1987 (bonus point if you got 1992 as well)
3. They are the only numbers of points not given from the 1-12 sequence
4. A: 66
5. C: 69
6. B: Moonlight
7. C: Money
8. ' . . . when northern lights are dancing'
9. Luxembourg, France Gall
10. Jemini

11. C. $900,000
12. B. Norway
13. C. Brighton
14. Dana and Dana International
15. A. Nicole
16. B. Eurocat
17. Stefania. Greece's performer was named Stefania, Ukraine's song was called 'Stefania'
18. A. 'Ooh Aah . . . Just A Little Bit'
19. Cornelia Jakobs was born in 1992, Destiny was born in 2002
20. B. SuRie

Credits

All Images © Shutterstock

06: Aussievision.net; Independent.co.uk; Tellymix.co.uk; Bbc.co.uk; Wikipedia.org; Variety.com
08: Wikipedia.org
10: Eurovision.tv; Wikipedia.org; Eurosong-contest.fandom.com
12: Wikipedia.org; Eurovisionworld.com; News.Sky.com; English.Alaraby.co.uk; ESCToday.com
14: Wikipedia.org; Eurosong-contest.fandom.com
16: Wikipedia.org; Eurovision.tv
18: Wikipedia.org; Eurovision.tv
20: Wikipedia.org; Eurovision.tv
22: Wikipedia.org; Nulpoints.net; Eurovision.tv
24: Wikipedia.org; Aussievision.net
26: Wikipedia.org; Aussievision.net; Digitalspy.com; Eurosong-contest.fandom.com
28: Wikipedia.org; Aussievision.net; News.com.au; Wiwibloggs.com; Eurovisiontimes.wordpress.com
30: Wikipedia.org; Eurovision.tv; Wiwibloggs.com; EscXtra.com; Aussievision.net; Ogaespain.com
32: ESCInsight.com; EscStats.com; Eurovision.tv; Eurosong-contest.fandom.com; Wiwibloggs.com
49: Wikipedia.org; themoscowtimes.com; Cnbc.com; Eurovision.tv; Radiotimes.com; Independent.co.uk; Timesofisrael.com; Wiwibloggs.com; Sbs.com.au; Fuzzable.com; Esctoday.com; Irishmirror.ie
50: Apple podcasts: The Official Eurovision Song Contest podcast
52: Wikipedia.org; Ian Winwood; *Kerrang!*, 2022
54: Wikipedia.org; Eurovisionary.com; Eurosong-contest.fandom.com; Nulpoints.net; Walesonline.co.uk
56: Wikipedia.org; aussievision.net; everyhit.com
58: Jeff Gordinier; *Entertainment Weekly*, 1996; Chrissy Iley; *Guardian*, 2007; The Jonathan Ross Show, ITV, 2013; Wikipedia.org; Britannica.com; Wiwibloggs.com; Smoothradio.com; Officialcharts.com; IMDB.com; Cbc.ca; Thesun.co.uk; Vox.com; Pollstar.com; Womansday.com
60: Wikipedia.org; Eurovision.tv; Bbc.com; Songfacts.com; Youtube.com
62: Wikipedia.org; Officialcharts.com; Aussievision.net; Reddit.com
64: Wikipedia.org; Eurovision.tv; EscXtra.com; Officialcharts.com; Udiscovermusic.com; Mundanemag.com; Flaunt.com; Twitter: Duncan Laurence
66: Wikipedia.org
68: Nick Duerden, *The Independent*, 2015; Brandon McCann, *ESC Daily*, 2014: Marta Jary and Monique Friedlander,

Daily Mail *Australia*, 2022; Booking.com, 2022; Wikipedia.org; Metro.co.uk

70: Daniel Welsh, *Huffington Post*, 2021; Steve Holden, Official Eurovision Podcast, 2022; Wikipedia.org; Eurovision.tv; EscXtra.com

72: Wikinews.org; Nulpoints.net; Eurosong-contest.fandom.com; Wiwibloggs.com; Eurovision.tv; Eurovisionworld.com; Rockdirt.com; Twitter.com

74: Wikipedia.org; Eurovoix.com

76: Wikipedia.org; Radiotimes.com

77: Eurovision.tv; Broadbandtvnews.com

78: Express.co.uk; Aussievision.net; Youtube.com

80: Wikipedia.org; Eurovision.tv

82: Dan Kois, *Slate*, 2020; Wikipedia.org; Eurovision.tv; Wiwibloggs.com; GQ-magazine.co.uk; EscXtra.com; Exberliner.com; Officialcharts.com; Music.allaccess.com

86: Wikipedia.org; EscXtra.com; BBC.co.uk; Eurovisionfam.com; Wired.co.uk; Sagepub.com; Rug.nl; Independent.ie; Walesonline.co.uk; Nationalworld.com; Towardsdatascience.com

88: Wikipedia.org; Metro.co.uk; Aussievision.net; Eurosong-contest.fandom.com; Independent.co.uk; Esctoday.com; Radiotimes.com; Youtube.com; Sbs.co.au

90: Daniel Welsh, *Huffington Post*, 2022; Wikipedia.org; Eurovision.tv; Alexanderrybak.com

92: Joebennett.net; CNN.com; Coyotepr.uk; Theconversation.com

94: Wikipedia.org; Eurosong-contest.fandom.com; Youtube.com

113: Daniel Rosney, Bbc.co.uk, 2022; Politicshome.com; Wiwibloggs.com; ESC-plus.com; Euronews.com; Kyivpost.com; Manchestereveningnews.co.uk

114: *The Big-Issue*, 2013; John Preston, *The Telegraph*, 2017; Fred Bronson, *Billboard Magazine*, 1999; Wikipedia.org; Officialcharts.com; Dailymail.co.uk; Playbill.com; Britannica.com; Judycraymer.com; Planetattractions.com; Abbaomnibus.net; Wiwibloggs.com; Dailystar.co.uk; Udiscovermusic.com; Forbes.com

116: 'Toy', written by Doron Medalie, Stav Beger, Jack White. 'You Are The Only One', written by Philipp Kirkorov, Dimitris Kontopoulos, John Ballard, Ralph Charlie. 'Fuego', written by Alex Papapconstantinou, Anderz Wrethov, Didrick, Geraldo Sandell, Viktor Svensson. 'El Diablo', written by Jimmy 'Joker' Thörnfeldt, Laurell Barker, Cleiton 'OXA', Thomas Stengaard. 'Nuku Pommiin', written by Jim Pembroke and Juice Leskinen. 'Golden Boy' written by Doron Medalie. 'Suus', written by Florent Boshnjaku. 'Dschinghis Khan', written by Ralph Siegel and Bernd Meinunger. 'Euro-Vision' written by Michel Moers, Dan Lacksman, Marc Moulin. 'Flying the Flag (For You)' by Russ Spencer, Morten Schjolin, Andrew Hill, Paul Tarry. 'Party for Everybody', written by Viktor Drobysh, Timofei Leontiev, Olga Tuktaryova, Mary Susan Applegate. 'Popular', written by Fredrik Kempe. 'Technicolour' written by Jessica Cerro and Dave Hammer

118: Wikipedia.org; Eurosong-contest.fandom.com; BBC.com; Escinsight.com; Aussievision.net; Irishtimes.com; Femalefirst.co.uk

122: '*Broadcasting House*', BBC Radio 4, 2022; Daniel Welsh, *Huffington Post*, 2022; Zoe Williams, *Guardian*, 2022; Wikipedia.org; Eurovision.tv; Mirror.co.uk; Recordoftheday.com

124: Dailymail.co.uk; Guinnessworldrecords.com; Thesun.co.uk; Smh.com.au

126: Wikipedia.org; Eurovision.tv

128: Eve Barlow, *Guardian*, 2018; Ugla Stefanía Kristjönudóttir Jónsdóttir, *Stylist*, 2022; Steve Brown, *Attitude*, 2018; Wikipedia.org; Timeout.com; Nbcnews.com

130: Daniel Welsh, *Huffington Post*, 2022; Roisin O'Connor, 2021, Zak Maoui; *GQ Magazine*, 2022, Wikipedia.org; Independent.co.uk; Wiwibloggs.com; Pride.com; Forbes.it

132: Wikipedia.org; Eurovision.tv

134: Mark Savage, Bbc.co.uk, 2022; Caroline Westbrook, *Metro*, 2016; Alex Nelson, Inews.co.uk, 2021

136: Daniel Welsh, *Huffington Post*, 2021; Lorraine, ITV, 2015; Jason Chester and Sarah Malm *Mailonline*, 2015; Mark Beaumont, The Independent, 2021; Dave Simpson, *Guardian*, 2016; *Wogan*, BBC1, 1986; Wikipedia.org; Eurosong-contest.fandom.com; Culture.fandom.com; Retropopmagazine.com; Youtube.com

138: Wikipedia.org; Eurovision.tv

140: Reddit, Netta: Ask Me Anything, 2019; Wikipedia.org; Guardian.com; Jpost.com; mirror.co.uk; Timeout.com

142: Wikipedia.org; Eurosong-contest.fandom.com; Express.co.uk; Youtube.com; Ilmessaggero.it